ON KNOWING GOD

ON KNOWING GOD

By
JERRY H. GILL

THE WESTMINSTER PRESS
Philadelphia

BOOK DESIGN BY DOROTHY ALDEN SMITH

First edition

Published by The Westminster Press ®
Philadelphia, Pennsylvania

PRINTED IN THE UNITED STATES OF AMERICA

9 8 7 6 5 4 3 2 1

Library of Congress Cataloging in Publication Data

Gill, Jerry H.
  On knowing God.

  Bibliography: p.
  Includes index.
  1. God—Knowableness. I. Title.
BT102.G54   231'.042   81-10481
ISBN 0-664-24380-0   AACR2

FOR
*The Fireside Group—
students, friends, family*

CONTENTS

(Continued)

Part Two
SHIFTING THE AXIS

Part Three

POST-CRITICAL PHILOSOPHY OF RELIGION

PREFACE

About ten years ago I wrote a book entitled *The Possibility of Religious Knowledge*. The present work represents the results of my continued wrestling with this same topic from an ever broadening and deepening perspective, and, it is hoped, a wiser one as well.

The working title for this present study was "The Heart Has Reasons," and in some ways I still prefer this phrase from Pascal, for it captures the central theme I am seeking to advance, that rationality is broader than most modern philosophers have allowed, while the heart is more reasonable than most existentialist thinkers have admitted. However, since I am especially concerned with the application of this theme to the possibility of knowing God, the present title is a happy choice.

I am greatly indebted to my students at Eastern College, on whom I tried the ideas in this book, for their patience and obstinacy. I am also very grateful to Professor Jack Rogers of Fuller Theological Seminary for his helpful suggestions and continued enthusiasm for my work. A special word of appreciation goes to Dr. James Heaney, who saw the manuscript through the labyrinthine process to final publication.

J.H.G.

INTRODUCTION

The plan of this book is simple. After focusing the chief characteristics of "critical philosophy," I shall sketch out the profile of a fresh perspective on the central concepts of modern philosophy and conclude by tracing the implications for the philosophy of religion. The overall aim is to provide a philosophical basis for religious epistemological claims which sets them free from the tyranny of the established way of approaching religious philosophy.

The defining characteristics of critical philosophy cluster around three concepts: experience, meaning, and knowledge. As an overall posture it is the legacy of Descartes, Hume, and Kant in the Enlightenment, and Russell, the young Wittgenstein, and A. J. Ayer in the twentieth century. *Experience* is viewed as essentially a passive encounter with discrete "objects" of physical reality. *Meaning* is defined in terms of a static, one-to-one relationship between objects and linguistic signs. *Knowledge* is based exclusively on an explicit process of inference from evidence to conclusion. Part One is devoted to the detailed presentation of this perspective.

The cutting edge of the above posture, indeed the point of the term "critical philosophy," is the assumption that all epistemological claims can and must be subjected to critical analysis in which the meaning of each and every term is rigorously specified and in which belief is never allowed to exceed objectifiable data and/or premises. In a word, the hallmark of critical philosophy is the demand that all aspects of experience, meaning, and knowledge be made explicit in a strict, rational sense. There are no reasons which reason knows not of.

The consequences of this approach for the philosophy of religion—as well as for all disciplines that deal with intangible dimensions of human experience—have been disastrous. For intangible reality is by definition out of the question for a philosophy that assumes the necessity and the possibility of making everything explicit. Whatever religious claims mean, it is clear that they involve the affirmation of a reality which in some sense transcends the observable and the explicit. Thus the present stalemate in the philosophy of religion.

Some have sought to overcome this standoff by advocating an existentialist posture in which religious belief is viewed as a matter of sheer commitment quite apart from any cognitive claims. In addition to finding this option basically irresponsible both philosophically and religiously—primarily because it provides no way of distinguishing between authentic commitment and credulity—I find it inadequate because generally it grants too much to established, critical philosophy. Simply to concede cognitivity, or to protest against its captivity at the hands of a narrow definition of reason by taking an irrationalist stance, is to fail to strike at the root of the difficulty. The very board on which the game has been played needs to be exchanged for a fresh one. Or, to change the metaphor (which is *not* merely a semantic triviality), the axis around which the issues orbit needs to be relocated.

My alteration of the epistemological axis of philosophy of religion is designated "post-critical," a term of Michael Polanyi's, in order to indicate that I am not advocating a naive, romanticist return to a classical/medieval perspective. The insights of modern thinkers are valuable in and of themselves; they only become insidious and debilitating when transformed into dogmas. This latter phenomenon can only be avoided by a thorough reconsideration of the *actual* character and shape of experience, meaning, and knowing. To put it pointedly, it is imperative not to lose sight of the fact that each of these dimensions of human existence can only take place *within* the space provided by certain factors which themselves cannot be explicitly analyzed and which are nevertheless embodied in the very act of rational analysis.

The fulcrum for effecting a relocation of the epistemological axis has been provided by three quite diverse contemporary thinkers whose works intertwine around the three major themes of experience, meaning, and knowledge. Merleau-Ponty's phenomenological explorations of experience, Wittgenstein's later investigations of language, and Michael Polanyi's insights concerning the personal and tacit foundations of knowing all combine to form a radically different epistemological fabric. I shall draw upon the contributions of these thinkers in Part Two, though my particular way of putting them together is my own responsibility.

The unifying motif that draws these thinkers and themes together is that of *active participation*. Each philosopher stresses the constitutive character of human participation in relation to the nature of experience, meaning, and knowledge. This motif runs absolutely contrary to the passive, static, and objectifying emphasis of critical philosophy. Post-critical philosophy acknowledges the *relational* and bedrock character of the structure of the human "form of life" or way of "being-in-the-world" and seeks to understand understanding by *accrediting* this relational involvement rather than viewing it as a form of contamination. It stresses the primordial and logically primitive quality of intentionality and trust in giving rise to knowledge, experience, and meaning.

All of this produces positive results for the philosophy of religion, results which I seek to draw together in Part Three. The crucial notions of revelation, God talk, and religious truth are interpreted in the light of the fresh point of departure provided by post-critical philosophy. Revelation and religious experience are treated as *mediated* in and through the other dimensions of reality. God talk is understood as multidimensional and *metaphoric* in nature, as neither "literal" nor "symbolic" but nevertheless cognitive. Religious truth is viewed as having an essentially *tacit* basis and structure, as would befit knowledge of mediated reality expressed metaphorically. Interpreting these crucial notions in this way liberates them from the confinement imposed by the self-negating dogmas of critical philosophy.

One way to get a handle on the significance of post-critical philosophy of religion is by means of Pascal's famous insight, "The heart has reasons which reason knows not of." This insight cuts two ways at once. Against critical philosophy it affirms and accredits the viability of truth which transcends the limits of rationality narrowly defined. In Polanyi's terms, "We know more than we can say." At the same time, and against most religious existentialism, Pascal's dictum acknowledges the necessity of distinguishing between *reasons* of the heart and *longings* of the heart. Only a post-critical philosophy can provide the framework within which reasons of the heart can be understood as epistemologically both responsible and revelatory.

It is important to bear in mind that the purpose of this study is not to establish the rationality of specific religious claims. It is, rather, to establish the rationality of religious claims in general. That is, its purpose is philosophical rather than apologetic, although the two are not unrelated concerns. The former constitutes a necessary condition of the latter. My own context, both culturally and personally, is specifically Christian and the focus of my efforts has been directed accordingly. Perhaps at a later date I shall be able to address myself to the apologetic task. Sufficient unto the day, however, are the difficulties thereof.

It may be argued, with a good deal of cogency, that critical philosophy as defined and traced in the pages of Part One no longer dominates the philosophical marketplace. In the twentieth century we are witnessing a general though gradual trend away from the assumptions of traditional modern thought. It is this trend which I am seeking to focus (especially in Part Two) and contribute to in this particular study. So far, little has been done by way of consolidating the insights and new directions suggested by such widely diverse "post-critical" thinkers as Maurice Merleau-Ponty, the later Wittgenstein, and Michael Polanyi. Moreover, next to nothing has been done by way of applying these insights and directions to the philosophy of religion. This is my purpose in Part Three.

Part One

CRITICAL PHILOSOPHY

1

THE PACKAGING
OF EXPERIENCE

In developing a post-critical philosophy of religion, one must first get clear as to the nature of "critical philosophy." Three central concepts for this dominant Western philosophical stance are experience, meaning, and knowledge. I shall treat these concepts in some detail, in the order mentioned, which would seem to be the natural or logical order. For one's concept of experience largely entails one's concept of meaning, which in turn largely entails one's concept of knowledge. To put it differently, it is experience that serves as the matrix out of which or within which meaning and knowledge arise. At the conclusion of this examination of critical philosophy I shall set out the consequences that flow from it for the philosophy of religion.

It is important to bear in mind that the characteristics under examination are not necessarily those which the thinkers comprising what is called critical philosophy *overtly* advocate. As often as not they function more as unarticulated presuppositions than as expressed emphases. This *covert* quality does not, however, render them any less important or dogmatic; in fact, it generally enhances these features. Thus the task at hand is a kind of "phenomenology of critical philosophy" in that it consists of surfacing those characteristics which constitute the critical philosophical stance, whether stated or only embodied. Another way of putting this is in terms of digging up what Stephen Pepper called the "root metaphors" out of which various philosophical approaches develop.[1] What are the root metaphors that underlie and inform critical philosophy?

EXPERIENCE AS ATOMISTIC

Perhaps the most pervasive common feature of all modern philosophy, whatever the particular movement or thinker, is the largely unstated assumption that experience is subject to *analysis* in terms of discernible *parts*. In fact, this assumption is so fundamental to our Western way of thinking and has proven itself so very helpful in such a wide range of circumstances that it is difficult to focus as an assumption at all. Indeed, the very activity of calling attention to it in the way that I am presently doing is parasitic on, or more correctly embodies, the assumption itself.

Part of this difficulty relates more directly to the nature and function of language, and thus will be more easily dealt with in the next chapter. It is worth noting that even this move, of dividing up the consideration of various aspects of a concept, presupposes the very analytic or atomistic characteristic of modern philosophy that is now under consideration. At the same time, it must be acknowledged that unless we are content to remain altogether silent about experience—as well as about everything else—we shall have to go ahead and speak as best we can. Moreover, the awareness of the reality of these difficulties goes a long way toward nullifying their pernicious effect.

The most obvious dimension of this atomistic perspective is simply the idea that experience comes packaged, as it were, in distinct, isolated parts. To put it slightly differently, critical philosophy assumes that experience consists of discrete particulars—as objects and/or substances which combine in various ways to form more complex aspects, but which at a fundamental level retain their independent existence. This view is helpfully referred to as *"atomistic"* because of its similarity to the models that used to be employed in atomic and subatomic physics. Experience is conceived of as comprised of "indestructible" units joined together in various molecular relationships which are either necessary, as with rationalism, or optional, as with empiricism.

Although rationalism and empiricism differ on many crucial issues, each in its own way shares in the atomistic perspective. The former school of thought considers reality to be essentially a thing of the mind and focuses on self-contained thoughts and/or ideas as the units of experience. Frequently rationalists speak of "the objects of thought" as though they were the furniture of the mind to be identified, arranged, and grouped by logical operations, but never broken down into smaller particulars. Empiricists, on the other hand, are well known for their commitment to "simple ideas" and/or "impressions," as with Locke and Hume, or to sense-data, as with twentieth-century thinkers such as Russell and Ayer. Such "perceptions" are spoken of as the building blocks of experience, grouped together through association in various "bundles," but ultimately self-contained in and of themselves.

Even though Kant's thought can be legitimately understood as transcending most of the difficulties attendant to rationalism and empiricism, as well as forming the basis for nearly all contemporary epistemology, his philosophy shares in this atomistic perspective as much as do the others. His initial definitions of "sensibility," "intuitions," and "concepts" on the opening page of *Critique of Pure Reason* make this abundantly clear, for from the very outset he speaks of "objects" giving us "representations" through the senses.[2] Moreover, his explanation of experience as a synthesis of perceptions and *a priori* categories consistently employs the notion of discrete "objects" as "represented" to our minds.[3]

A second important dimension of the atomistic perspective functions as a corollary of viewing experience as coming in distinct, independent units. It is the almost always unspoken presupposition that in addition to, and perhaps *because of,* being constituted of isolated particulars, experience can be *described* and/or analyzed in terms of particulars *without distortion.* Almost without exception, and especially since the development of modern philosophy, no matter where or whom one reads there seems to be a complete lack of awareness of the possibility that breaking experience down into individual units might somehow do violence to the structure of experience itself. Although it does not necessarily follow that analysis of experience will produce a distorted account and understanding of it, the possibility ought not go unacknowledged.

Beginning with Descartes and moving on down through Hume, Kant, Mill, Russell, the early Wittgenstein, and Ayer (as well as through lesser lights), one is continually struck by what can only be described as philosophical naiveté with regard to the potentiality of an analytical approach to experience actually obscuring its character. Only with the advent of pragmatism and phenomenology do we find philosophers who not only display an awareness of the difficulties inherent in the analytic stance but seek to develop an approach that will avoid them. The later insights of Wittgenstein also reveal a concern for such a posture. But more of this in Part Two.

Actually, it is not simply the idea that atomistic analysis predetermines and perhaps falsifies our understanding of experience which is problematic. For there are instances in which such an approach serves a good purpose. The real difficulty lies in the lack of awareness that *any* analysis of experience can only be carried on within the framework or context provided by a specific task or orientation, that there is no such thing as "neutral" or "given" units of experience.

The root metaphors upon which critical philosophy is based are drawn from the sciences, both formal and natural, as they were conceived in the Enlightenment and Newtonian era. Not only are there other orientations that might and do yield different accounts of experience, but contemporary science is no longer bound by the paradigms and metaphors that underlay the Newtonian approach. Thus atomism is now out of vogue in the natural sciences, and there are even signs that the behavioral sciences, except for behaviorism, are turning elsewhere for direction and orientation.

A third salient aspect of the atomistic view of experience is its inherent *reductionism*. If we assume that experience actually comes divided up into discrete units, not only may our analysis of it in such terms distort our understanding of it but we will be led quite naturally to assume that a full account of the individual parts will necessarily provide us with an explanation of the whole of experience. Just as molecules are said to be fully explained by, or exist as a function of, the atoms comprising them, so experience and/or its various aspects and dimensions will be thought to be exhausted by an analysis of the so-called "objects" of sensation or thought.

Such reductionism is clearly at work in nearly all philosophies of the modern era, and it is especially characteristic of the analytic or critical perspective. The early moderns, such as Descartes,[4] Hume,[5] and Kant, exhibited reductionistic tendencies quite clearly. They explained all experience in terms of either simple concepts, simple ideas (sensations), or a combination of both. Even Kant reduces it to a synthesis of intellectual "categories," sensory "intuitions," and sense-data.[6] Twentieth-century thinkers, such as Russell,[7] Ayer,[8] and the young Wittgenstein,[9] assume they have given an exhaustive account of experience and/or reality when they have discussed the nature of perceptions, objects, and the relationships between them. Anything other then these factors either does not exist, is not experienced, or cannot be spoken about.

EXPERIENCE AS MENTALISTIC

It comes as no surprise to those familiar with rationalist thought that a major characteristic of modern philosophy is that it treats experience almost exclusively in terms of mental phenomena, ideas and minds. Although the ideas of extension and solidity do have their place in thinkers such as Descartes, Spinoza, Leibniz, and Hegel, it is *as ideas* that they are dealt with, not as physical realities in their own right. The body, with its sensory and motor faculties, is given a kind of begrudged, second-class citizenship among rationalists.[10] Experience and knowledge are strictly functions of ideas and the coherence among them.

On the other hand, it may seem surprising to suggest that even empiricist thought is essentially mentalistic in nature. For the hallmark that is supposed to distinguish empiricism from rationalism is its reliance on the physical senses to provide knowledge of the world outside the mind. Nevertheless, it remains the case that it is exceedingly difficult, if not impossible, to maintain a "realist" form of empiricism against the difficulties inherent in the "egocentric predicament," as the idealism of Bishop Berkeley and the phenomenalism of Hume, together with contemporary sense-data theorists, make frustratingly clear. Perceptions are, after all, according to empiricist definition, mental phenomena.[11] Moreover, the quotations from Kant in the notes to the previous section clearly exhibit his mentalistic tendencies as well. For him the phenomenal world of experience is the result of mental representations structured by the categories of the understanding. The noumenal world of "things in themselves," outside our minds, is unknowable.

The logic of beginning with a representational theory of experience, as does empiricism, would seem to lead inexorably to some form of idealism. For, although the definition of truth for empiricists is a *correspondence* between our ideas and/or sensations and the extramental world, the fact that the test for truth must be some form of *coherence* among present, previous, and possible sensory representations renders the concept of nonmental experience quite out of the question. The only other tack is to argue, as some phenomenalists do, for the incorrigibility of bedrock sensory judgments ("protocol statements") such as "green," "here," "now." And there is hardly any question as to the basic mentalistic character of the experience giving rise to such judgments.

One of the most remarkable features of modern philosophy's mentalism, and one that is especially characteristic of the emphasis here being termed "critical philosophy," is the all but complete lack of attention given to the *body* when offering an account of human experience. The fact that our experience is uniquely and always an embodied one is only taken to mean that the body somehow serves as a kind of connection device between what is thought to be the external world and our minds. At best it transmits representations to our minds, while at worst it stands forever between us and the world, distorting our understanding.

Often, as with Descartes and Hume, our experience of the physical world is said to be logically dependent upon our mental experience, and this seems to include our knowledge of our own bodies. Descartes, for instance, moves *from* his insight "I *think,* therefore I am" *to* the conclusion that he exists in space, in spite of the fact that while engaged in working all this out he relied upon—indeed, thought by means of—his bodily skills, physiological processes, and interaction with his physical environment. More recent thinkers have given even less attention to the physical dimension of experience, except those working within the pragmatist and phenomenologist schools of thought. Such considerations are generally dismissed as "matters for psychology," not philosophy.

Yet another facet of the mentalism endemic to critical philosophy is brought out by considering the fact that from within this posture all experience is, at the most fundamental level, a *function of interpretation.* The data that our minds receive are in and of themselves neutral and disconnected; they stand in need of being ordered by our rational or mental faculties. Descartes, Hume, and Kant all placed the responsibility on the mind for transforming the "blooming, buzzing, confusion" of supposed "raw data" into some sort of experienceable form. Contemporary critical philosophers of the phenomenalist sort have gone so far as to conclude that physical objects, including our own bodies, are nothing but "logical constructs"[12] formulated by our minds as a means of dealing with the vast array of sensations we encounter.

Perhaps the most interesting case in point with respect to this tendency to view experience as a function of intellectual interpretation is the debate over our knowledge of other minds. From a critical philosophy point of view, the existence of minds other than our own is problematic because it depends upon our drawing an inference from our own observed behavior being correlated with our own mental activity and our observations of other persons' behavior.[13] We are said to infer or interpret that their behavior is correlated with mental activity unique to them. Once again a representational approach to perception can be seen to entail a mentalistic or intellectualist understanding of experience.

One final aspect of this mentalistic motif bears mentioning. It must not be overlooked that both the content and the form of critical philosophy's perspective are *abstractive* in nature. That is to say, the reductionistic account of experience in terms of isolated units of sensation or thought necessarily implies that all compound and/or complex features of experience, such as chairs, table, and persons, are in actuality *abstractions* (logical constructs) which go beyond experience.[14] Thus the content of the view can be said to be abstractive. At the same time, and more important for present purposes, the critical account of experience in terms of sense-data (simple ideas, impressions, etc.) is itself an abstraction in the sense that our experience *as experienced* is not comprised of such atomistic building blocks. We have primarily to do with "middle-sized" phenomena, and concepts of sense-data, etc., are as abstract as are those of nations, negative numbers, and concepts themselves. Thus to explain the world in terms of such notions is itself to participate in a highly intellectualist approach to the understanding of experience.

EXPERIENCE AS STATIC AND PASSIVE

There are two further characteristics of critical philosophy that have figured into the discussion of the previous two, albeit in a minor or background fashion. They are, however, features that deserve to be brought to the fore because they are generally overlooked altogether.[15] In addition, they are helpfully considered in tandem because they tend to reinforce each other. The two characteristics are *staticity* and *passivity*. Together with atomism and mentalism, they provide the framework within which critical philosophy takes shape. In the next and final section of this chapter I shall trace out the broad outlines of this shape or ontological posture.

The pervasive yet often unnoticed static quality of experience, as envisioned by critical philosophy, can be seen in the fact that the various aspects of experience are thought of as *mutually independent,* not only of one another but in relation to the observer as well. That is to say, the relationships between and among the particulars said to comprise experience are assumed to be constant and essentially arbitrary or optional. Moreover, there is no dynamic between that which is known or experienced and the person who is doing the knowing or experiencing. Thus, according to this view everything is what it is in and of itself, and relationships are rather accidental in the first place, remaining static once established. Relationships do, of course, change, but not in themselves; only when particulars are rearranged do relationships alter, and then only as functions of the particulars. In a word, relationships—indeed, change itself—have no dynamic of their own, they are static.

Another way to put this is to say that for critical philosophy the various atomistic features of experience are not only disconnected and mutually independent, but they are essentially *neutral*. That is, they have no natural inclinations or affinities for one another, nor are they in any way dependent upon or affected by coming into relationship with perceivers. There is no interaction between that which is apprehended and the "prehender" (to borrow a term from Whitehead). Thus each thing, each datum or quality, is simply what it is, quite apart from what other things are and where it stands vis-à-vis those others.

Once again this quality of critical philosophy can be seen as pertaining both to its content and to its form. Not only is the world it describes essentially devoid of process and interaction, but the description itself is offered as a completely objective and neutral account, as if the giver and the receiver of the description were not participants in the world—and as if giving and receiving descriptions were not aspects of experience. To assume that the features of experience are fundamentally neutral toward one another, and that one can describe them, much as one would take a snapshot, without interacting with them, is to assume that experience is static.

Closely related to the notion of staticity is that of passivity. Within the purview of critical philosophy, experience is understood as something that is *received* or "had." The experiencer receives or is confronted by the elements or atoms of experience as if they paraded by on a television screen or simply bombarded the senses like sound waves. The "blank tablet" notion central to empiricism is familiar enough, but the same passivity is reflected in rationalist thought with respect to the manner in which ideas are experienced. For ideas are said to be perceived "clearly and distinctly" by "the natural light of reason," as with Descartes, or to be "received" from and "given" by the senses ("yielding concepts"), as with Kant. Contemporary atomists tend to speak of "stimuli" and "input" being "taken in" or "scanned." Although Kant spoke of the role of the mind in constructing experienced reality, it remains true that he paid almost no attention to the role of the active body in relation to the world.

Not only, then, are the elements of experience conceived of by critical philosophy as passive in nature, as having no "vectorial" (directional) relationships among themselves, but the observer is also conceived of as being aware of them in a strictly passive, noninteractive fashion. The possibility that we must, or even can, be engaged with or geared into the various dimensions of experience in order to experience them at all never so much as enters into the critical picture. In fact, any such active involvement is generally considered to be a necessary evil at best and as necessarily eliminable at worst. A crucial element in the standard definition of "objectivity" is thus seen to be passivity. A good account of experience will, of course, be an objective, therefore passive, one.

Perhaps there is no more pointed and thoroughgoing embodiment of these two closely related features of critical philosophy than that found in the early Wittgenstein's *Tractatus Logico-Philosophicus*.[16] Although there are significant differences between this position and those of other modern philosophers, there is also a way in which the *Tractatus* stands as a paradigm case of the more important characteristics of critical philosophy. It clearly exhibits atomistic and mentalistic emphases as well as those of staticity and passivity. The root metaphors of the *Tractatus* are logical space and logical mirroring. "Atomic facts" are said to exist in logical space, with all of the relationships among them being represented by propositions. A proposition is said to demarcate a place in logical space and this place is then thought of as a "logical place." Thus place is parallel to point in geometry. Moreover, all places in logical space bear a relationship to one another, a relationship that can be thought of as a network of lines joining points in space. Once a proposition has designated a place in logical space, the whole network is in effect laid out, because space is both finite and determinant.

The metaphor of logical space carries with it a visual perspective, and that in two senses. *Within* the view thereby espoused, the relationship between reality and thought (as well as language) is said to be one of "picturing." The latter pictures the former. Sometimes the imagery shifts to "mirroring," but the implications remain the same. Also, *as* the view is espoused, the relationship between it and the speaker (Wittgenstein) together with the hearer is a visual one. We are asked to *see* the relationship between language and reality in much the same way as we would a vast but definite, perhaps two-dimensional, space populated by points joined by lines, in a gridlike fashion. We are not placed within this space, but view it from outside.

It is clear that there is no action or movement within logical space; it is static. Points remain constant and the connections among them do so as well. This is not to say that Wittgenstein maintained that language and

reality do not change and/or evolve. It is just that he was not interested in
the dynamics of and between language and reality. He was, rather,
interested in their formal nature. In any given state, at any given instant,
the relationships are what they are and from one instant to the next their
logical character remains the same. In addition, once again we are on the
outside of this world. There are no speakers or hearers in logical space; there
is no interaction, for Wittgenstein apparently thought that such
considerations were unimportant to an understanding of language.

EXPERIENCE AS REALMISTIC

The foregoing characteristics of critical philosophy combine together to
form an identifiable ontological posture, which for lack of a better name I
shall call "realmism." Prior to modern times the standard, pre-critical view
of experienced reality saw it as dualistic in nature. In general, the world and
our experience were thought to be divided into two main realms—the one
natural, tangible, and transitory; the other transcendent, spiritual, and
eternal. The classical perspective, following Plato, interpreted these realms
philosophically, while the medieval perspective, following Augustine and
Aquinas, viewed them theologically. The primary thrust of modern
philosophy in general and critical philosophy in particular has been to deny
the existence of a transcendent realm, and thus to interpret all human
experience as natural and tangible.[17] All vertical relationships have been
translated into horizontal ones.

In almost every field of thought the major debates have centered around
the defending or negating of the reality of a transcendent realm of human
experience. Generally the view that maintains the homogenous, natural
character of experience has been the most persuasive and thus pervasive.
Idealists and existentialists have gradually given way to positivists and
Marxists. Critical philosophy, as an ontological stance, takes shape in this
context. It may be viewed as both a contributing cause and an effect of the
development of *naturalism*.

Perhaps the central ontological dogma of critical philosophy is
reductionism, the belief that all aspects of experienced reality, including
those which seem transcendent in character, are reducible to or explainable
in terms of the natural, observable level of human experience. Sometimes
this dogma is referred to as "nothing-but-ism" because in one form or
another (A is *only* B, X is *merely* Y, etc.) it consistently asserts that all cases

in which there appears to be a transcendent element are nothing but extensions of the natural realm. Materialists claim that all intangibles are nothing but epiphenomena, positivists argue that all value judgments are nothing but expressions of emotion, behaviorists maintain that mind and spirit are nothing but conditioned behavior, and Marxists affirm that culture and society are nothing but reflections of material conditions.

The debate over reductionism is widely known. What is *not* widely understood is that in spite of the disagreements between those who affirm two realms and those who deny a transcendent realm both sides agree at a more fundamental level. For both sides carry on the debate within the common assumption that experienced reality *must* be understood in terms of realms, whether one, two, or more. In other words, no one questions the advisability, let alone the viability, of intepreting experience according to a realm or level model.

While dualism and reductionism share the responsibility for the dominance of realmism in the history of Western philosophy, it is critical philosophy with which we have to do, and that for two reasons. First, it is critical philosophy, as the contemporary and focal thrust of reductionism, which is replacing dualism as the established position. Second, the burden of proof lies with critical philosophy because it makes an essentially negative claim in denying the existence of a transcendent realm. To put it differently, the actual reduction of all aspects of experience has yet to be accomplished; indeed, it is not even on the horizon.

The most powerful point of connection between the salient characteristics of critical philosophy and reductionism lies within the concept of atomism. For to believe that experience comes packaged in terms of self-contained units which combine in optional, molecular relationships with one another to form more complex aspects of experience *is* to be committed to reductionism from the outset. Of course dualism also generally buys into atomism, but it usually does so by maintaining two distinct kinds of experiential units, each corresponding to its appropriate realm. In both schools of thought the idea that experience might have a nonatomistic and nonrealmistic structure goes entirely unexplored. In Part Two, I shall offer an initial exploration of this possibility in terms of the notions of *mediated* dimensions and relationships.

The other point of direct connection between critical philosophy and reductionism has to do with their shared emphasis on the static and passive character of experience. For if the aspects of experience have no dynamic inherent within themselves and their interrelationships, and if the relationship between them and the prehender is essentially a noninteractive one, then of course there is nowhere else to turn for an explanation of experience as a whole but to the individual constituents themselves.[18] The whole of experience is simply the sum of its parts. If, however, the structure of experience can be shown to have a dynamic and active character, then reductionism and critical philosophy can be overcome. But more of this in Part Two.

One final matter. It should again be acknowledged that in the twentieth century a number of philosophical movements have arisen to challenge the packaging of experience offered up by critical philosophy. Pragmatism, phenomenology (excluding Husserl, who was something of a positivist and an atomist), and ordinary language philosophy all tend to be more oriented toward a flexible contextual, relational understanding of experience. In Part Two, I shall draw on these schools of thought in constructing a "post-critical" approach. It should also be noted again, however, that little has been done to work out the implications of these emphases for the philosophy of religion; thus the rationale for Part Three of the present work.

2

LANGUAGE
AS REPRESENTATION

There exists an appropriate parallel between critical philosophy's approach
to experience and its approach to language. Language is, after all, our way
of expressing our experience, so it is not surprising that our interpretation
of the one would befit our understanding of the other. Although it is
generally assumed that theories of experience are logically prior to theories
of language, largely because it is presupposed that experience itself is more
fundamental than language, there are at least some reasons for suggesting
that the dependency actually runs the other way. It is possible that language
is *constitutive* of experience as much as it is expressive of it. This, however, is
not the place to enter into such a discussion. Suffice it to say that in general
there is a parallel between one's theories of experience and language, and
critical philosophy is no exception.

A helpful way to characterize the overall position of critical philosophy
with respect to the nature of language is to say that it has a *representational*
view. The point of this way of speaking is to call attention to the emphasis
on the idea that language *stands for* or *refers to* the various elements of
experience in a one-to-one relationship. The main features of this position
are that: (1) words name things, (2) sentences picture states of affairs, (3)
meaning is ascertained by analyzing the structure and referential quality of
sentences, and (4) absolute precision is the ultimate goal of language. I shall
discuss these features in this order, making clear as the discussion
progresses how they parallel those of critical philosophy's approach to
experience.

WORDS NAME THINGS

There is something very commonsensical about the idea that words
function as labels for the elements of experienced reality. Children seem to

31

begin speaking by pointing to things and saying their names. We learn second languages by memorizing long lists of words that stand for objects in the world. The logical extension of this idea is parodied by Jonathan Swift's people who carry miniature objects around with them in huge sacks and speak by setting various ones out for their "hearer" to see. In a more serious vein S. I. Hayakawa and others have generated a worldwide movement, known as General Semantics, around the notion that language is a map of reality, wherein each word stands for a spot in our physical and social landscape.

The history of this representational idea of language is difficult to trace, for not many philosophers prior to the twentieth century took account of the importance and nature of language. Generally the naming, or "luggage tag," theory of linguistic expression seems to have been active, if not dominant, from the outset. Both Plato[1] and Aristotle[2] speak about, and more important, *use*, words as if they were names, as do Augustine,[3] Aquinas,[4] and even such moderns as Descartes,[5] Hume,[6] and Kant.[7] Bishop Berkeley, in his preface to his *Principles of Human Knowledge,* acknowledges that such a view of language is clearly naive,[8] but he then proceeds to go right ahead and employ it in working out his idealistic philosophy. In the twentieth century the idea became a foundation stone in the scientific philosophy of the Vienna Circle[9] and in the empiricism of British philosophers such as Russell[10] and A. J. Ayer.[11]

There are those who argue that the real source of this understanding lies in the grammatical structure of Indo-European languages, especially Greek. The subject/predicate pattern is said to presuppose and/or entail a naming relationship between words and things. The main grammatical category is the noun (a *name* of a person, place, or thing), since even the action described by verbs must be done by a subject (which is named by a noun). Verbs themselves could be thought of as names for actions. Those who argue in this way usually go on to suggest that there are other languages in the world which do not have a noun-centered grammatical structure (many are verb-centered) and that such languages might be better suited to certain linguistic tasks, such as those appropriate to subatomic physics and the social sciences.[12]

Be that as it may, the fact remains that critical philosophy, as the dominant motif of modern and contemporary philosophical thought, bases its understanding of language on the idea that the essential function of words is to name the objects in human experience and/or the relationships well-defined and highly influential criterion for distinguishing meaningful from nonmeaningful utterances. If one defines meaning in terms of the picturing of states of affairs, then the criterion for meaningfulness will necessarily be whether or not a given utterance does serve as a picture of experienced reality. There are two senses of "does serve" which need to be sorted out. On the one hand, an utterance may seek to picture a state of affairs and do so incorrectly, in which case the result is a false picture, but nonetheless a picture just the same. In this case the utterance does *not* serve as a picture of the *actual* state of affairs, but it *does* serve as a picture of a *possible* state of affairs; it is, then, a meaningful utterance.

On the other hand, an utterance may *appear* to picture a state of affairs, but may in fact picture neither an actual nor a possible state of affairs. That is, on the surface level it may look as though its grammatical and referential functions are similar to those of utterances which do picture facts, but closer examination reveals that they are not. This type of utterance does not serve as a picture of experienced reality because it is not really a picture at all; it is, then, a nonmeaningful utterance. Incidentally, there is a third classification—namely, those utterances which express logical relationships and as such are devoid of factual content. These do not picture actual or possible states of affairs, but are still meaningful in a specialized sense (they are either tautologies or contradictions).

A handy way of summing up the above ideas and distinctions is in terms of the notion of *verifiability*.[18] The test for the meaningfulness of a given statement turns out to be whether or not it pictures at least a possible state of affairs, and the way to determine this is to ask, "Does the statement make a claim which in principle could be shown to be either true or false?" In a word, "Is the statement verifiable?" If a statement does not make such a claim, it cannot be said to picture either an actual or a possible state of affairs, and thus cannot be said to be meaningful. To put it differently, if there is no way to establish, in principle, whether a statement is true or false, it is not making a claim and is not serving as a picture of experienced reality. This approach to meaning has come to be known as "the verifiability criterion of meaning."

The consequences of applying this criterion, as critical philosophy has done (whether in an implicit fashion, as with the early empiricists or in an explicit form, as with the logical positivists), are as crucial as they are far-reaching. The general result has been to eliminate from the realm of meaningful discourse whole disciplines which traditionally have been accepted as having to do with getting at the truth about the world. Metaphysics has been dismissed, and theology along with it, as failing to meet the verifiability criterion, since no agreed-upon method of determining the truth or falsity of its statements has been or can be arrived at. Ethics and aesthetics have also been set aside as not being of interest philosophically because they deal exclusively in subjective value judgments which do not picture states of affairs, since there is no established way to determine the truth or falsity of the utterances typical of them.

One way of summarizing the consequences of the pervasive employment of critical philosophy's verifiability criterion of meaning is in terms of the notion of cognitivity. The criterion, because it focuses on the question of verifiability, can be said to divide all statements into two kinds, those which are cognitive in nature because they are subject to judgments of truth and falsity, and those which are noncognitive since they do not. Cognitive statements seek to picture experience, while noncognitive utterances do not. The latter are generally said to be "emotive" in nature because they serve to express and/or direct emotions and actions rather than mirror reality. There is a strong parallel between the traditional distinction between objective statements, which are factual and/or logical in nature, and subjective statements on the one hand and this contemporary distinction between cognitive and noncognitive utterances. Critical philosophy can be said to generate and endorse both.

Before this section is concluded, it should be acknowledged that the verifiability criterion has undergone a good deal of refinement, and has even been publicly abandoned, since its original arrival on the scene in the work of Russell, the early Wittgenstein, and A. J. Ayer.[19] The fact remains, however, that in spite of these refinements and verbal abandonments, the spirit of the criterion continues to dominate contemporary philosophical activity. Not only are there those who still advocate a hard-nosed, analytic empiricism based on a kind of logical atomism, but even among those who are generally thought to be beyond such narrowness there often remains an unstated assumption that language stands over against experience in some kind of representational manner and that its meaning is a function of this relationship. This assumption reveals itself more in the *way* these thinkers do philosophy than in the views they assert and defend. It is this spirit which continues to animate and nurture critical philosophy.

which do not have meaning, and (3) to teach others how to tell the difference.[20]

PRECISION AS AN ABSOLUTE

The notion of precision runs as a minor theme throughout each of the previous sections of this chapter. It is now time to bring it to center stage in order to round out our consideration of critical philosophy's theory of language. Behind the naming theory of words stands the idea of an *exact* one-to-one correspondence between words and things. Behind the picture theory of meaning stands the concept of a *perfect* mirroring of states of affairs. Behind the commitment to analysis as the means of ascertaining meaning stands the notion of a *complete* analysis. These "behind the scenes" emphases join together to form the goal of absolute precision in all linguistic expression.

To begin with, critical philosophy contends that absolute precision is *necessary* to the fulfillment of meaning. The argument runs like this. Unless both the speaker and the listener are perfectly clear as to the exact meaning (i.e., referents and syntax) of the utterance in question, they cannot be said to be talking about the same thing. Although it is possible to get by without absolute precision, because we can rely on assumed commonalities of experience and convention, some features of the meaning involved will be lost and/or confused. When pressed, as we are in some situations, to be more exacting, we often cannot agree, and communication breaks down. Thus precision is necessary to full and serious communication.

This argument is considerably intensified when placed within a scientific or philosophical context. It is not possible to make progress in either of these fields without defining key terms, if not all relevant terms, carefully and exactly. The same can be said for such fields as jurisprudence, business, and sports, although to a lesser degree. In any situation where distinctions and judgments are the order of the day, it is necessary to have precise definitions in order to accomplish the tasks at hand. Ambiguity and vagueness only and always lead to confusion, misunderstanding, and frequently to misfortune.

Precision has been at the forefront of philosophical concerns from the very beginning. Socrates continually pressed for more exactness with respect to common yet crucial terms, Plato's theory of Forms can be seen primarily as a way of ensuring precision of meaning, and Aristotle was forever making distinctions among the many senses of important terms. The medieval philosophers, together with the moderns (Descartes through Kant), took it upon themselves to define their key terms carefully before embarking on their investigations. The nineteenth century saw a considerable laxness with respect to precision, but twentieth-century thinkers, especially of the critical variety, have gone a long way toward restoring the concern for precision to its place of centrality in philosophical endeavor.

The other side of the coin with respect to precision as a goal in linguistic expression is the contention that not only is exactness necessary to full and serious communication, but it is *possible* as well. Clearly, to argue for the necessity of precision is to assume that it is possible to achieve it. Critical philosophy can be understood as pressing for both the necessity and the possibility of precision, and indeed as frequently offering itself as an example of it.[21] Although the notions of necessity and possibility are closely related to each other, they often warrant separate treatment. Since the concern for necessity has been introduced, a brief account of possibility is in order.

As has been mentioned, the notion of the potential for absolute precision has functioned more at the presupposition level than at the conscious level. Perhaps it can best be highlighted through a presentation of the skeptical argument against it. There are those who argue that it is impossible to obtain absolute precision linguistically because of the relativity which accompanies both the contexts within which we learn to speak and the accumulated associations of our individual mental processes. No two people *ever* mean exactly the same thing by any terms they use. Therefore, communication, in the sense of meaning the same thing, is never possible. Precision *is* necessary to communication and meaning, but it is also impossible to achieve.

Critical philosophy seeks to counter this argument by pointing out that precision of meaning is not a matter of two or more people having the same thing "in their minds" when communicating by means of a given term. It is, rather, a matter of abiding by the *same definition* of the term in question. Moreover, the relativity which results from the fact that we all learn the meaning of terms in slightly different contexts can be overcome by fresh, mutually agreed upon stipulative definitions. Granted that in most cases people do fail to communicate, or do so in a sloppy manner, the demand for absolute precision can minimize, if not eliminate, this unfortunate situation. Only by insisting on both the necessity and the possibility of absolute precision can we achieve and maintain full communication.

I shall return to this debate in Chapter 6. The present chapter would not be complete, however, if we failed to consider the logical extension of critical philosophy's concern with precision as an absolute. I refer to the development of ideal or *artificial languages* as a means of obtaining this requirement. Beginning with Russell and Whitehead's *Principia Mathematica* and on up through Rudolf Carnap's *Logical Syntax of Language* there has been a continual effort on the part of critical philosophers to invent full-blown nonnatural ideal languages from which all ambiguity and vagueness are eliminated. The general plan is to define each and every term in the language, either in terms of others, or in terms of logical operations, or in terms of ostensive definitions (i.e., pointing at the object in question). By using the latter as the foundation stones which actually have incorrigible contact with the ground of experience, and by moving up the abstraction ladder only in terms of carefully defined rules, one can arrive at an absolutely precise language which functions as a closed system.[22]

The suggestion of critical philosophers is that by substituting such a language for the hybrid of natural language terms and mathematical symbols presently used by science, great progress could be made. Ideally they would like to think it possible to replace natural languages altogether, but such dreams have consistently run aground on both practical and theoretic considerations. Not the least of the latter has to do with the seeming necessity of developing and communicating the intricacies of the artificial language to others within the limitations of the only other languages already available—namely, natural ones. I shall use this difficulty as a jumping-off point for the considerations of Chapter 6.

3

KNOWLEDGE
BY INFERENCE

This presentation of the main features of critical philosophy would hardly be complete without due consideration being given to its approach to the question of knowledge. In many ways epistemology constitutes the very heart of the critical posture and tends to encompass, or at least imply, its stand with respect to experience and language. The main concern of the critical approach to epistemology is to establish the *inferential process* as the only sound method of acquiring knowledge. The nature and the basis of this position should become clear as a result of the following considerations.

TRUTH AS EGALITARIAN

The critical approach to knowledge had as its initial purpose the liberation of the search for truth from the confines of the *authoritarian* and/or esoteric monopoly which characterized previous societies. Socrates, Plato, and Aristotle, together with some of their forerunners, sought to overcome static, traditional points of view on what was true by emphasizing the necessity of *giving reasons,* which were accessible to everyone, to substantiate truth claims. Francis Bacon, Descartes, Spinoza, and Locke, along with the pioneers of science, strove to set knowledge free from the restrictions imposed by the medieval practice of thinking *within* certain established theological and philosophical ideas.

Another tradition against which critical philosophy labored was that of mysticism, according to which truth about important things was available only to those who fulfilled certain rather arbitrary conditions—and such truth was self-authenticating. Both rationalists and empiricists wanted to establish an egalitarian basis for knowledge which required only that a person be able to bring common powers of reason to bear on openly specified evidence and/or premises. According to modern, critical thinkers there are no self-authenticating *truths*, though there are, as we shall soon see, self-authenticating or incorrigible *experiences*. Each and every claim to knowledge must be subjected to analysis and evaluation. Explicit inferential processes provide the only proper criterion by which the tyranny of authoritarianism and mysticism can be overcome.

Rationalists such as Descartes and Spinoza developed *deductive* inference, patterned after geometry, as the means of establishing truth beyond the strictures of authority and mystical intuition. They argued that absolute certainty could be reached only by beginning with self-evident "axioms" and moving flawlessly by deduction from one conclusion to the next. Empiricists such as Locke, Hume, Mill, and Russell won out as the spokesmen for critical philosophy because they advocated *inductive* inference, pointing out that deductive inference itself rests upon a form of intuition. What is self-evident to one person may not be so to another. Inductive inference, by contrast, begins with the data of sensory observation and aims not at certainty but at high probability.

The inferential process, whether deductive or inductive, establishes knowledge as a *mediate* phenomenon rather than an immediate one. Thus it allows critical philosophy to take up a middle position between skepticism and mysticism. It can affirm the actuality of knowledge without guaranteeing it. Moreover, it brings the means of knowledge out into the public arena, making it accessible to everyone with normal reasoning abilities. More pointedly, inductive inference bases itself in the data of experience rather than in the creative or intuitive powers of the mind and is therefore more available for analysis and evaluation. Also, in redefining knowledge in terms of high probabilities, empiricism opened the way for a stronger connection between critical philosophy and science.

While Kant's epistemology seeks to form a synthesis of rationalism and empiricism, it can also be seen as stressing the inferential process. Kant extolled inductive inference with respect to the content of natural science, while advocating "transcendental" inference with respect to its form. By basing such crucial concepts as time, space, and causation in "the categories of the understanding" he sought to establish them beyond the limitations of simple empirical investigation but short of the content-oriented absolutism of rationalism. The "critical process" which constitutes the heart of Kant's epistemology is yet another example of the effort to ground knowledge in an inferential process.

Contemporary critical philosophers have pretty much rejected the transcendental aspects of Kant's approach, along with the notion of *a priori* synthetic knowledge (especially in mathematics). They follow Hume more closely than anyone, but Kant's critique of metaphysics as an unwarranted extension of the categories of the understanding beyond their capabilities is always incorporated into critical thought.[1] With this goes a general skepticism concerning offering any justification of the categories themselves, or of the inferential process as such. To be sure, some thinkers do seek to develop a completely pragmatic justification,[2] usually couched in terms of probabilities, but most are content to accept the process by which we obtain knowledge as a matter of convention and/or survival. Some critical philosophers still hold out for a skeptical posture, claiming that there *can* be no justification for inferential processes, and thus none is needed.[3]

INCORRIGIBILITY AND DOUBT

There are two central concerns inherent in the critical approach to knowledge, and both pertain to the task of finding a reliable point of departure or foundation for a sound epistemology. If the superstructure of knowledge claims is going to be viable, it would seem that it must be grounded in a manner that is beyond dispute; the individual claims themselves will only be as reliable as the basis upon which they rely. Furthermore, if questions can be raised about the authenticity of the first move, there is no hope of constructing an epistemology that can rise above the attacks of skepticism. What is needed is an indubitable starting point. This is critical philosophy's first concern.

It is well known that Descartes and other rationalists sought to ground their epistemological efforts in self-evident truths which would function much as axioms do in geometry. Generally these self-evident propositions were taken to be the logical outgrowth of the definitions of their key terms, such as "substance," "thought," "existence," etc. The ideas embodied in these terms were thought to carry with them, or "in" them, certain truths that could not be denied without giving rise to self-contradiction. Sometimes these ideas themselves were said to be already in the mind; at other times only such principles as noncontradiction, sufficient reason, and the like were claimed to be innate.[4]

There are two notorious difficulties connected with this approach to incorrigibility. One is the simple fact that what is self-evident to one person frequently will not seem so to another. As a classic case in point, consider that in spite of agreeing on the essentials of their common approach, Descartes ended up a dualist (mind and body), Spinoza a monist (pantheist) and Leibniz a pluralist (an infinite number of "monads"). The second difficulty is that it is pretty well agreed today that logical principles and definitions are devoid of factual content, or what logicians call "existential import." In other words, principles such as noncontradiction yield strictly analytical truths which are unable to tell us anything about the actual world. "All bachelors are married" is self-contradictory, but this does not tell us whether or not there *are* any bachelors.

For these and other reasons the empiricists, like Locke and Hume, sought an indubitable starting point for their epistemological efforts by grounding them in simple sensory impressions. They argued that if one begins with such primitive perceptions and moves on only to ideas and conclusions that can be exhaustively traced back to them, then one will be able to arrive at reliable knowledge. Simple sensory impressions were thought to provide a bedrock, inerrant link between reality and the human mind. All our knowledge of the world was said to derive from sensory experience, with neither ideas nor principles being innate. It is well known, however, that Locke did not make a clear break with rationalism, nor with medieval thought, and that Hume himself raised questions about the empiricist posture which undermined its confidence concerning the certainty that sensory impressions derive from outside the mind.[5]

Contemporary empiricism has managed to drop all ties with the past and has overcome Hume's skepticism by refusing to affirm the connection between sensory impressions and the external world. Taking up a more guarded position, known as "phenomenalism," current empiricists are content to claim, following Kant, that our knowledge is limited to the content and structure of our minds—and that this is sufficient for both common sense and science. By building on incorrigible sense-data observations (incorrigible, not because they reveal the truth about the external world, but because they cannot be subjected to criticism or corrected—who can tell another person that he is *not* having such and such sensations?), and carefully weighing the evidence at every step, reliable knowledge is available. It is this updated empiricism which best exemplifies contemporary critical philosophy.[6]

The second central epistemological concern of critical philosophy has been with the proper method of discovering this indubitable beginning point. Both rationalism and empiricism, each in its own way, employed the method of *doubt* as the primary guide in this search. Descartes reasoned that the only way to be sure that a candidate for self-evidency is trustworthy is to attempt to doubt it. If one can doubt it, or deny it without self-contradiction, then it is not a self-evident truth. If, on the other hand, a proposition that cannot be doubted or denied can be found, then an epistemological bedrock has been uncovered.[7] In this way the method of doubt became an important feature of critical philosophy.

Hume, on the other hand, employed doubt in a slightly different manner. He presupposed, without ever saying it in so many words, that for a knowledge claim to be veridical it must have an adequate form of support, and that each and every form of support must in turn have an *adequate rational basis.*[8] Thus to question or doubt every claim to knowledge was the only way to ascertain its reliability; every assertion is thus "guilty," or at best neutral, until proven trustworthy. It is in this form that doubt has become the cutting edge of critical philosophy, and indeed the dominant epistemological posture of the twentieth century.

As has been mentioned, Kant's epistemology has been incorporated into critical philosophy at crucial junctures, allowing it to overcome, or at least sidestep, certain key difficulties. One such difficulty was that of making sure that our sensory impressions actually resulted from and/or represented the world external to our minds and thereby provided an incorrigible point of departure for our system of knowledge. Kant's philosophy sought to show that although the structure of the human mind, focused in the categories of thought, made it logically impossible for us to know about the reliability of our experience as a guide to reality, as long as we only claim to have knowledge about our experience we do in fact have an indubitable epistemological base. Our minds, which fortunately are structured similarly, both limit and facilitate our knowledge in the areas where we need it.[9] Thus the phenomenalist stance of critical philosophy.

A second difficulty which Kant's philosophy helps deal with is that of the fruitfulness of systematic doubt as a method of establishing a sound beginning point for knowledge. Many philosophers object, with Kierkegaard, that teaching a person to think by first teaching the person to doubt is like teaching someone to stand up straight by first teaching the person to lie down in a heap. Kant's approach actually begins at the other end from Descartes and Hume. He reasoned that since we already have knowledge—witness common sense and science—our task is not to doubt its possibility until it can be established, but rather to ascertain what must be the case since it already is a reality.[10] Some critical philosophers have incorporated this more "positive" stance into their thought, but they interpret this epistemological confidence as a function of practicality and convention, and not as a source of knowledge about the world apart from the human mind.

ANALYSIS AND ARTICULATION

In Chapter 1 critical philosophy's emphasis on the analysis of experience into its simplest constituent parts was introduced and developed. When we turn to a consideration of critical epistemology we once again are confronted with the centrality of *analysis*. Just as each aspect of experience was identified and characterized as a separate and distinct entity in the atomistic approach, so each line of support and each move from one to the next in the inferential process must be located, scrutinized, and evaluated. Descartes's *Discourse on Method* has as its major theme the breaking down of every argument into its component parts and evaluating each before going on to the next. Spinoza tried to improve on Descartes by defining all his terms and specifying his axioms at the outset, and then proceeding to deduce all of his propositions from them. Although empiricists followed a more inductive procedure, they too sought to separate and evaluate the various steps of every line of support offered on behalf of knowledge claims.

Contemporary critical philosophy employs the sophisticated machinery of modern symbolic logic to analyze the individual claims and arguments involved in current epistemological discussion. The very use of such devices embodies a commitment to an analytic understanding of the inferential process, for it presupposes that the various phases of a line of reasoning can—and *must*—be amenable to being designated by individual symbols and operations. Actually, the very notion of inferential knowledge itself would seem to carry with it the necessity and possibility of such analysis and symbolization. Generally this approach to the field of epistemological endeavor is itself assumed rather than supported—and when it is supported it is presupposed that *its* support must be inferential and analytic in nature.

A parallel, though often unnoticed, notion to that of the analysis of lines of reasoning is that of *articulation*. Not only does critical philosophy maintain that each step in a reasoning process must be identified and scrutinized, but this analysis must be explicitly articulated so that other persons can follow and evaluate the process for themselves. Thus the concern for explication is not just to ensure the veracity of each step for the original seeker of knowledge, but it is also a way of helping others to share in that search. Of course, not the least of the advantages of this sharing is the possibility of corroboration and/or disvalidation of the original process itself. Articulation, therefore, provides a kind of public check-and-balance system for critical epistemological investigation.

Perhaps the chief characteristic of knowledge by inference as conceived of in critical philosophy is that of *reversibility*. By specifying and analyzing each part and each step of the reasoning process it becomes possible to move either from premises and data to conclusions or from conclusions back to premises and data. Once each phase of the process has been articulated, it becomes possible exhaustively to explicate all that goes into a line of reasoning and thus to leave nothing unsaid or merely implied. This characteristic of reversibility not only has become a major theme in critical philosophy's epistemological stance but it has become a dominant emphasis in the entire academic enterprise as well. How frequently students receive comments on their papers such as, "These are the correct answers, but I want to see your work" or "until you can articulate your reasons for your views, you cannot be said to know them."

This stress on articulation and reversibility goes a long way toward guarding against confusing a lucky guess or correct opinion with true knowledge. Plato made the case well for the value of distinguishing between knowing that a certain road leads to a specified place because one has traversed the road and affirming that it does so on someone else's authority. But there are two problems which such an emphasis gives rise to and does not solve. One is simply that no single individual can ever travel down every road. Without being able to take other people's word for things, we would be able to know precious little. Second, there is a built-in assumption in all this that it is always possible to articulate the reasons for a particular knowledge claim. If people continually get the right answer even though they cannot say how or why, as with calculating prodigies, are we prepared to deny them the use of the word "knowledge"? I shall return to these issues in Chapter 7.

The profundity and complexity of the emphasis on articulation becomes apparent when one raises the question about the justification of the inferential process itself; what sort of support can be given for *it*? [11] Hume raised this question in a most pointed fashion when he sought for the foundations of inductive knowledge. He concluded that the inferential process as applied to experience was dependent on the assumption that the future will be like the past—the uniformity of nature. The only justification that can be offered for this assumption is that in the past the future has been like the past, which is clearly circular reasoning. Thus Hume concluded that there is no rational justification for inductive inference. We use it because we can do no other; but this is a matter of psychology, not philosophy.

Kant realized that it is somehow inappropriate to seek the justification of the reasoning process outside the process itself. He argued that the inferential process is part of the makeup of the human mind and justifies itself in the thinking process itself. The phenomenal world, within which we make inductive inferences, is *defined* by the categories of the mind and thus inference is legitimate within these bounds. It is not legitimate, however, with respect to the noumenal world (things as they *are*, independent of the mind), because the categories by definition do not extend that far. The early Wittgenstein took essentially the same position, although transposed into a linguistic format, except that he realized the inconsistency of talking about the noumena at all. Therefore, he concluded the *Tractatus* by repudiating his own distinctions, but only *after* establishing them. He wanted to keep his cake and eat it too.

More contemporary critical philosophers often seek a strictly *pragmatic* justification of inductive inference. That is to say, they argue that although no ultimate, self-sustaining support can be given for engaging in the inferential process, if we do make inferences and the future turns out to be like the past, we have knowledge, while if we do not make inferences, we shall not have knowledge whether or not the future turns out to be like the past. We have everything to gain and nothing to lose.[12] Aside from sounding strangely circular, this tack makes it sound as if we could choose *not* to make inferences, which would be difficult to imagine.

Whichever posture is adopted by various critical philosophers, they all agree in insisting on the cruciality of the inferential process and the full articulation of each of its steps. This cruciality would seem to apply even to the justification of the process itself, although not unproblematically.

OBJECTIVITY

A final important aspect of critical philosophy's overall epistemological position is the stress on *objectivity*. In a sense the previous emphases on inference, analysis, and articulation all lead up to and are encapsulated in this notion. Moreover, it is a notion that has become something of a watchword for the contemporary mind-set in nearly every field of endeavor. One even finds it bandied about in the world of commercial advertising, to say nothing of journalism, labor arbitration, and science fiction. Of course the philosophical use of the concept has a more refined focus than does the popular.

Perhaps the most important feature of the critical concept of objectivity is the stress on the elimination of all personal, or subjective, factors from the process of ascertaining what is true in a given situation. Personal factors, sometimes called "value judgments," are those which pertain to the knower rather than to what is known. For critical philosophy the epistemological goal is to keep our knowledge of experienced reality as pure as possible, to know the world as it is apart from our experience of it. Although it is generally admitted that such purity is not obtainable, the presumption is that the closer it can be approximated, the more reliable will be the knowledge. Subjective factors are regarded as a kind of "contamination," and are minimized and guarded against as carefully as possible.

One of the most thoroughgoing and influential expressions of such objectivism is that of Laplace. He epitomized the modern critical dream when he claimed that if he were given *all* factual data, the complete state of the universe at any given instant, he would be able to describe both the complete future as well as the entire past of the whole universe.[13] Although the notion of a closed, Newtonian universe, upon which Laplace based his claim, has been repudiated in contemporary times, the dream still holds sway among critical philosophers. One highly influential and characteristic expression can be found in the thought of Karl Popper, who contends that it is entirely possible as well as desirable to define knowledge as if no knower were involved at all. This is the burden of his essay "Epistemology Without a Knowing Subject."[14]

It is not always made clear just what is meant by "subjective factors" and/or "value judgments." At least three fairly distinct kinds of things need to be distinguished. The first is simply the personal desires and hopes of the investigator. Our knowledge must not be patterned according to what we would like the case to be, whether for reasons of comfort, reputation, or gain. Secondly, objectivism aims at a description of the facts, indeed a definition of "fact," which is completely free of theoretical interpretation. Theories must be based on data, not vice versa. Thirdly, by objective is meant a description of the way things are quite apart from the activity of the describer.

Critical philosophy generally affirms the elimination of all three of these forms of subjectivity from its account of the meaning and basis of knowledge. Although it acknowledges the impossibility of completely eliminating the second and third forms, it remains committed to such elimination as a defining characteristic of knowledge and as a goal to be striven for. On the credit side it is not difficult to see the importance of this commitment as a way of overcoming the human tendency to believe that what we *wish* were the case is *in fact* the case. On the debit side, however, it must also be admitted that there are serious conceptual difficulties attendant to the notion of knowledge as independent of theoretic and participatory considerations, even as an ideal.

Another way this concern for objectivity is frequently put is in terms of a knowledge claim being able to stand on its own, supported only by the facts. But it is problematic as to what exactly this means, let alone whether it is possible. There is serious question as to whether there are such things as "facts" apart from the perspective supplied by a theoretic framework of some sort.[15] Furthermore, recent developments in the history of science and sociology of knowledge[16] indicate that personal and sociopolitical factors are essential rather than detrimental to the acquisition of knowledge. Finally, the extension of Heisenberg's principle of indeterminacy to forms of knowledge other than subatomic physics has highlighted rather than diminished the role of the knower in defining the known. This will be discussed in Chapter 7.

One other aspect of the approach of critical philosophy to epistemological theory bears mentioning before this chapter is brought to a close. Out of the constellation formed by all of the foregoing emphases has come a kind of *epistemological ethic* which characterizes both critical philosophy as such and the areas of contemporary society which have been particularly influenced by it. Some have termed it "the modern morality of knowledge."[17] Put simply, it consists in the idea that it is essentially irresponsible for persons to believe or commit themselves to a proposition or point of view beyond what the evidence supports. As Locke put it, we must make our beliefs "proportionate to the evidence."[18] W. K. Clifford's essay "The Ethics of Belief" is the *locus classicus* for this perspective as it applies to the philosophy of religion.[19]

The degree to which we, as "critical moderns," are committed to this epistemological imperative can be measured by the degree to which we are offended by Pascal's proposal concerning religious faith. He suggested that if we are having difficulty believing, we should try behaving *as if* we do—going to Mass, kneeling in prayer, singing hymns, etc.—and see if we do not take on faith through participating in it.[20] According to critical philosophy, this proposal is not only misguided, it is immoral. For one must not believe, or even act as if one believes, until *after* one *knows*. Knowledge and faith are necessarily in opposition for critical philosophy.

4

THE CONSEQUENCES
FOR RELIGION

It is time now to draw together the religious consequences of the foregoing characteristics of critical philosophy. The importance of this task should by now be evident. For the development of the philosophy of religion in modern times, though less so in recent years, has taken place largely within the rubrics derived from the critical understanding of experience, language, and knowledge as set forth in the preceding chapters. Moreover, even where this has not been the case, little attention has been paid to focusing the assumptions to be overcome. In this chapter, I shall present the specifics of this development for the concepts of religious experience, God talk, and religious truth, in that order. This will complete our overview of critical philosophy, together with its implications for the philosophy of religion.

RELIGIOUS EXPERIENCE

It will be recalled that the critical view of human experience is in many respects a *denial* of the traditional dualism espoused by classical philosophy and theology. It seeks to establish a one-level, naturalistic understanding of experience in place of a two-level, natural/divine dichotomized view. As has been pointed out, this way of drawing the lines of opposition is entirely dependent on a "realmistic" view of reality in which the various aspects of experience are thought of as quite distinct from, if not opposed to, one another. Both dualism and naturalism presuppose this realmistic model, the former arguing for two realms and the latter arguing for one.

This way of approaching the question of the nature of experience in general predetermines the options available for dealing with the notion of religious experience and/or revelation in particular. Essentially there are but two ways to go: either one holds out for the traditional view (epitomized in Augustine and Aquinas) of religious experience as in some way being an encounter with the "higher" or divine realm by persons living primarily in the natural realm, or one "goes modern" and interprets religious experience as an awareness of an additional factor totally within the natural order. It is my contention that nearly every thinker who has sought to treat religious experience in anything like a positive manner has done so in one or the other of these ways, without seriously questioning the realmistic model upon which they both are based. More important, it seems clear that neither of these options can overcome the criticisms of the idea of religious experience generated by critical philosophy, unsurprisingly and specifically *because* they share in the realmistic model at the foundational level.

According to a dualistic approach,[1] religious experience must be viewed fundamentally as an *intrusion* of the divine into the natural world. The stress is upon discontinuity between the two realms, and any encounter with divinity constitutes a disruption and to some degree a negation of the natural order. In an effort to establish the reality of the religious and the veracity of the experience of it, those who take this approach generally find themselves having to stress the bizarre character of the experience. Thus mystical encounters, scientific miracles, healings, and visions become the stock-in-trade of this way of understanding religious experience, whether one is dealing with "general revelation" (that available to all humankind) or with "special revelation" (that available through specific, historical circumstances).

The chief difficulty with this dualistic approach is this: In spite of the fact that the divine realm, for which such thinkers are contending, is said to be "above" and "other" than the natural realm, the attempt to establish its reality and character inevitably hinges on the employment of criteria that are derived *from* the natural realm. For if the divine realm *completely* transcends this world, then we would not be able to recognize it when we encountered it—or to distinguish it from simply going mad, chaos, or whatever. Yet, once criteria are employed to enable us to make such recognitions and distinctions, they can only be criteria that are derived from the natural realm. (Unless, of course, the criteria are as much a gift of God as the revelation itself—in which case the same situation holds: either there are some natural criteria by which to evaluate these divine criteria, or we are left with a skepticism.) Thus, either religious experience escapes us entirely, meeting no criteria that we can employ, or it is simply reduced to yet another element within the natural world. Even here, it is often, if not almost always, said to fail to meet the criteria suggested.

Another way of putting this difficulty is in terms of the *atomism* inherent in modern, critical philosophy. Once one has bought into the idea that experience comes in totally distinguishable and independent parts, then one is hard-pressed to locate or identify a religious or divine aspect of experience without falling into the trap of seeking to *isolate* it from the rest of experience. Either one is unable to do this, because the divine transcends the naturalistic categories available for isolation, or one successfully isolates the divine in terms of the "miraculous," only to find that at best religious experience has been reduced to such naturalistic categories as the bizarre, the powerful, or the unexplainable, which is hardly satisfactory from a religious point of view. At the worst, individual claims are merely rejected as not meeting any of these categories. In any case, the assumption that all features of experience can be identified in isolation leads the notion of religious experience down a blind alley.

If, on the other hand, one chooses the option of interpreting religious experience as simply an awareness of an additional feature within the natural realm,[2] the results are no better. For it is difficult (if not impossible) to make a case for a religious element within a totally natural world while operating under the assumption that the various aspects of experience can be isolated from one another by atomistic analysis. Once a person consents to this criterion, the burden of proof rests with that person to specify the particular aspect meant, distinguishing it clearly from all other features. One will either fail in this project, or succeed at the cost of having naturalists ask why they should bother to employ a special category, such as "religious," in order to refer to what is perfectly well treated under such rubrics as psychology, sociology, biology, political science, economics, history, etc. With Laplace it will be said that theism "is an hypotheses for which there is no need."

In addition to the difficulties which the "realmism" and atomism of critical philosophy cause for the concept of religious experience, there is also a problem which derives from its inherent *mentalism*. Generally speaking, those thinkers who have sought to develop a positive approach to the possibility of religious experience and revelation have done so within the confines of a view of human understanding which renders human experience a static, passive, *reception* of or *exposure* to certain data. At best some of these thinkers view experience as a function of intellectual interpretation. In either case, religious encounter and revelation are usually conceived of as internal, "spiritual" phenomena which are "taken in" or which happen as the result of having received or been confronted by certain data or ideas.

The reason such a view raises difficulty is that it leads almost directly to the position that faith is essentially a matter of intellectual assent to certain ideas, facts, or propositions. For, if the religious or divine comes before us much as images on a television screen, then faith must be thought of as an acceptance of the veridical nature of these images. This has been the dominant view of faith up until contemporary times and its connection, though not its insemination, with critical philosophy's understanding of experience ought by now to be fairly clear. The current alternative to this view of faith is that offered by existentialist theologians who make faith essentially a matter of individual *commitment*. The move here is to overcome one one-sided view by proposing yet another. What is needed, it seems to me, is a *relational* understanding of religious experience and faith which goes beyond both the passive mentalism of critical philosophy and the "volitionalism" of existentialist thought. More of this in Part Three.

An excellent example of the sort of difficulties and dilemmas discussed above can be found in the book that recently stirred up a good deal of ruckus, *The Myth of God Incarnate*.[3] Offering what is essentially a naturalistic interpretation of Christian revelation, it seeks to employ the criteria of the natural realm and maintain the special significance of the idea of the incarnation at the same time. The pivotal failure of the book lies in its inconsistent stand with respect to the realmism which it presupposes. On the one hand the authors repudiate the traditional idea of a supernatural realm from which God intrudes via the incarnation into our natural world. At the same time, they insist that in some undefined way God is "active" in the natural realm. The "reality" of the divine in the natural world remains unspecified and unisolated, thereby failing to meet the proper and accepted naturalistic criteria. Once again we are confronted with the problem of insisting on *keeping* our cake and *eating* it too.

GOD TALK

Just as the view of language in critical philosophy goes hand in glove with its interpretation of experience (the former as a picture of the atomic facts of the latter), so the two go together when it comes to tracing out the consequences of critical philosophy for religious thought. When religious experience is thought of as an isolatable encounter with an intrusion from a higher realm, religious language will appropriately be viewed as consisting of names and pictures of the elements comprising that which is encountered. Not only has this been the traditional understanding of God talk, but even today, perhaps because of the dominance of critical philosophy, it continues to be the standard view of both the person in the street and the majority of philosophical thinkers. The majority of theologians have rejected this interpretation of religious language in favor of an existentialistic "symbolic" view. I shall treat each of these approaches in turn.

A straightforward "naming" theory of religious and theological words follows both from traditional philosophy and theology *and* from modern critical thought. It is safe to say that aside from a few Deists and Transcendentalists those who have worked in the area of philosophy of religion, whether pro or con, have presupposed that to speak of God, heaven, hell, and the incarnation is to speak of persons, places, and events in essentially the same way as we speak of Henry VIII, England, and the Civil War.

In fact, theologians have spent an enormous amount of time collecting, examining, and discussing the significance of the various names and qualities of the separate members of the Godhead. Furthermore, they have generally treated such concepts as divine election, redemption, and judgment as events transpiring in the spiritual realm, essentially like events in the natural realm only on a grander scale. In the same vein, the various relationships and interactions that comprise religious reality are nearly always dealt with as metaphysical or theological "facts" which can be and are "pictured" by God talk. Theology is therefore understood as a kind of *superscience* in which the data gathered about the divine realm are expressed in as straightforward language as possible, some of which is borrowed from language appropriate to the natural realm, while some is said to be unique to the supernatural realm.[4]

By and large, modern philosophers have spent their time denying the existence of the persons, places, and events said to be named and pictured by religious language. They have argued either that the assertions which affirm the reality of these entities are false, in that they do not accurately picture reality, or that they are misguided in that they do not refer to any reality at all. In either case, these philosophers too have assumed the naming and picturing function of God talk.[5]

The twentieth century, however, has brought a shift in focus with respect to the nature of critical philosophy's attack on religious language. Because of the refinement of the picture theory of meaning, critical philosophy no longer maintains that talk of God and other religious phenomena is false; they now argue that it is *meaningless,* by virtue of the fact that it does not in actuality seek to picture facts at all. The verifiability criterion of meaning, when applied to God talk, necessitates that religious speakers indicate the means by which their statements might possibly be shown to be true or false. Until such means are specified, God talk and all other forms of religious language can only be judged as cognitively meaningless.[6]

There are roughly three main responses that have been made to the verifiability criterion as applied to religion by those who continue to take God talk seriously. One is to accept the consequences of these critical insights and look for other forms of meaning for God talk to have. Some have suggested that religious language functions as a mode of expression for human *value commitments.*[7] A second response is to maintain that God talk *meets* the verifiability criterion, since at death and/or the final judgment we shall find out whether or not the facts or states of affairs which it pictures are real. Thus it is meaningful, even if it turns out to be false.[8] This response, like the first one mentioned, does not question the appropriateness of the verifiability criterion with respect to religious language.

A third, and more prevalent, response to the challenge of critical philosophy involves the outright denial of the applicability of verifiability to God talk. Generally those who make this move maintain that all talk of religious reality must be understood as symbolic in nature. This posture can be expressive of either an idealist position or an existentialist position. The former is pretty much out of vogue today, its place being taken by process philosophy and theology. Existentialist theology, on the other hand, especially of the Bultmannian and Tillichian varieties, is still very much at center stage and deserves a closer look.

The Bultmannian approach[9] denies the dualism of the two-realm ontology at the outset. Thus it appropriately drops the picture theory of meaning with respect to religious talk as well. While accrediting the viability of the atomistic nature of experience and the picturing function of language for the natural realm, the only realm there is, Bultmannians interpret God talk as existentially but not cognitively significant. It expresses our personal commitments *within,* not beyond, the natural realm. Thus all religious language needs to be "translated" out of its factual mode into its existential mode. For it symbolizes our values and self-understanding *mythologically*. In this way the challenge of critical philosophy is sidestepped, but the basic understanding of the function of language goes unchallenged.

The Tillichian approach[10] does not deny the dualism of the two-realm ontology, but it argues that only a symbolic interpretation of God talk has viability with respect to the spiritual realm of reality. The language appropriate to the natural realm is said to be composed of *signs,* whereas that befitting the spiritual realm consists of *symbols.* The former represents or pictures, in an arbitrary fashion, the facts of physical reality, while the latter are said to participate, in an organic way, in the spiritual reality of which they speak. Although the verifiability criterion is deemed appropriate to the natural realm, it does not apply to the spiritual realm. In addition to the fact that this approach readily accepts the realmistic interpretation of experienced reality and the picture theory of meaning without challenge, it also fails to provide an adequate characterization of and criterion for discerning the significance of symbolic meaning.[11]

All in all, the consequences for philosophy of religion of the critical approach to language have produced an unbridgeable dichotomy between (1) a flat, simplistic interpretation of God talk, one that either deprives religious language of its mystery or renders it erroneous, and (2) a mythological or symbolic interpretation which leaves it both vague and unrelated to the language of the natural world. This dilemma can only be overcome by completely altering the common views of experience and language which form the axis of *both* of these approaches and starting over from a fresh angle. This task will be addressed in Parts Two and Three of the present study, where I shall draw heavily from the insights of a different branch of analytic philosophy—namely, "ordinary language analysis."

RELIGIOUS KNOWLEDGE

Critical philosophy began, as a focused movement, with Descartes and rationalism. As will be recalled, this form of critical philosophy sought absolute certainty by beginning with what appeared to be self-evident, indubitable, premises and moving ahead by strict, deductive inference. The empiricist form of critical philosophy, on the other hand, sought and continues to seek high probabilities by beginning with incorrigible sensory observations and moving ahead by inductive inference. In both cases, the *inferential process* serves as the crucial characteristic, for it is what distinguishes modern critical thought from classical and medieval thought by making the search for knowledge a public, accessible process which is subject to review and evaluation. In this section I shall trace the ramifications of this dominant motif for the concept of religious knowledge.

It was the stress on deductive certainty which gave rise to what have come to be known as "the classical proofs of God's existence." Although Aquinas, and Anselm before him, constructed such arguments for proving the existence of God, it was only with the modern rationalists that the character of this approach became clear. There is serious question as to whether Anselm and even Aquinas construed their respective constructions as proofs *per se,* but there is no question that they have been interpreted as such in the history of the philosophy of religion. Their purpose has been to provide a fully articulate, objective basis for the very heart of religious knowledge—namely, knowledge of God.

The key, of course, to the strength as well as the weakness of these so-called proofs lies in their proposed self-evident beginning point. Generally speaking, it is difficult at best to find fault with the deductive reasoning of thinkers such as Aquinas, Descartes, Spinoza, and even Hartshorne. The never-ending interest in and problem with these arguments focuses on the key terms and/or concepts from which they seek to "squeeze," as it were, the certain knowledge which they claim to afford. The whole case rests, finally, on being able to draw the existence or reality of God out of original and commonly accepted definitions of such terms as "perfection," "first cause," "necessary cause," and "sufficient cause."

The three primary criticisms of this overall approach to religious knowledge have pretty well rendered it unfruitful for the contemporary mind. The first is simply that deduction is itself a process that is devoid of knowledge about the world. It is a powerful but *empty system* of thought which can yield knowledge only when fed data from experience. Secondly, definitions do not pertain to questions of existence, they only provide *proposals* for and/or *reports* on linguistic usage. We must not confuse concepts with facts. Thirdly, even if such proofs were to be established as valid, it is very doubtful whether this could be thought of as a viable form of religious knowledge. Somehow finding God at the end of a syllogism leaves a great deal to be desired. Deductive inference does not hold much, if any, promise for those interested in knowledge of divine reality.

The empiricist approach to religious knowledge has emphasized the *experiential* basis of the inferential process. The two main kinds of experience that have been stressed are historical miracle and personal encounter. The Biblical record of the miraculous activity of God in the history of the Hebrews and the Christian church has been proposed and defended as strong evidence for the conclusion that God has been and can be known. In addition, other historical witnesses, both written and oral, to *miracles,* such as those at Lourdes, have been offered as evidence that God exists and is active in our world. The second kind of evidence brought to bear is that of the *personal experiences* of the millions of people who have and do claim some sort of interaction with the divine reality in their daily lives. Religious encounter has always been an important part of human life, whether in preliterate or literate cultures, and it is difficult to discount or explain away such a universal and powerful phenomenon.

Some of those who argue for the viability of religious knowledge on the basis of experiential evidence pursue the incorrigibility theme of critical philosophy in a very direct manner. They contend that there is no rational justification for doubting the *direct experiential report* of another person. Because it is impossible for one person to deny another's claim to perceive what the first person does not, it is equally impossible for nonreligious people to deny the claim that religious people make when they say they know God. Aside from the rather obvious difficulties with these proposed parallels between sensory observations such as "green," "here," "now" and religious claims of experience with God (the latter clearly involves a greater degree of interpretation), it is apparent that this experiential approach buys into the assumption that knowledge is somehow the objective result of an articulatable inferential process. Thus this approach clearly participates in the critical philosophy posture.

The chief difficulty with basing an understanding of religious knowledge on inductive inference does not lie in the fact that such an approach fails to provide certain knowledge. Rather, it lies in the presupposition that knowledge in general, and knowledge of divine reality in particular, consists in a totally explicit, fully objective, intellectual process. This is not the place to go into a full critique of the view that knowledge comes only by inference. That must wait for Chapters 7 and 11. Suffice it to point out at this juncture that the efforts of the empiricist school of thought have yet to deliver what was promised.[12]

An incorrigible, perceptual point of departure has never been established. All experience takes place in some context and is to some degree a function of interpretation. Complete objectivity is not only a practical impossibility, it is a theoretic one as well. Only within a strictly defined context can one hope for anything like complete articulation and precision—and even then it is never absolutely complete. Moreover, the defining of the context cannot be strict until *it* is placed within a precisely defined context itself, *ad infinitum.* In other words, if *every* step of the process needs to be articulated *before* knowledge can result, then we can never get started. Finally, if it is irresponsible to commit ourselves beyond what the inductive inferential process fully justifies, then we are consigned to a life of almost complete inactivity.

If religious knowledge is thought of as being grounded in inductive inference alone, it is subject to all of the above difficulties. For this reason many thinkers working in the philosophy of religion have opted for a voluntaristic basis of religious knowledge—or for an outright rejection of knowledge in religion altogether. This existentialist posture thus seeks to sidestep the intellectualism inherent in any inferentially oriented approach, thereby making religion more a function of life and commitment. Some of these thinkers speak as if a "leap of faith" or a commitment of will leads to a kind of mystical certainty of divine reality and/or God. Others drop all mention of the possibility of *knowing* God at all, preferring to speak of faith and/or belief as sufficient for the religious life. This position is a kind of "religious skepticism" or "committed agnosticism."

The main difficulty with this response to the dilemmas presented by the standoff between the rationalist and empiricist approaches is, as has been mentioned before, that it provides no way to distinguish between responsible and irresponsible commitment. This is a problem with respect to evaluating another person's commitment, for although we are not called upon to *judge* other persons, we do need to be *discerning,* since we live (both as persons and as religious folk) in community. But it is a crucial problem even for each individual in relation to her or his own commitment, for one cannot pledge allegiance to every claim that comes down the pike. Some are mutually contradictory, and some are downright debilitating. So the existentialist approach only *reinforces* the dead-end quality of the consequences of critical philosophy for the philosophy of religion.

Reason Versus Faith

One way of summarizing the net result of following the approach to the philosophy of religion entailed by critical philosophy is in terms of the distinction between reason and faith. Traditionally the relationship between these two central concepts was one of *necessary harmony,* if not outright identity or equation. With the advent of modern critical thought there came a dividing of the ways. On the one side stood those who endeavored to employ the insights of critical philosophy to maintain the harmonious relationship between reason and faith. They saw faith as the natural outgrowth of or response to the conclusions of reason, whether deductively or inductively conceived. Modern idealism, Deism, and Transcendentalism, and liberalism followed this path.

On the other side stood those who saw critical philosophy as driving a wedge between reason and faith, rendering their relationship one of *necessary opposition.* Religious faith was now interpreted as irresponsible credulity by most of those advocating a "modern" stance. Bertrand Russell is a dramatic case in point. These were joined as well by those who agreed that reason and faith are necessarily opposed but who saw this opposition as providing a solid basis for a fresh understanding of faith as existential commitment. They would say with Kant's words, though not necessarily with his meaning, that they had "set aside reason to make room for faith."

The stalemate resulting from the demise of the traditional harmony on the one hand and the standoff between contemporary empiricism and existentialism on the other pretty well spells the death of the philosophy of religion. The only alternative approach which has been seriously considered is that which advocates a *complete separation* between reason and faith while stressing the importance of each in its own way. Unlike traditional forms of this posture, such as that of Aquinas in which reason and faith were given separate fields of inquiry, the contemporary form tends to view reason and faith as two distinct ways of looking at the same phenomena. One can either take one and leave the other, or preferably affirm both at the same time, but neither as harmonious nor as opposed, simply as different. It is difficult to overestimate the increasing popularity of this approach, especially among theological thinkers.

While having a number of things to be said for it as a way past the difficulties resulting from the above-mentioned views, this approach still leaves us in a dichotomized situation. Only now the dichotomy is internal, not external, producing a kind of schizophrenia. Moreover, this approach tends to play fast and loose with the cognitivity dimension of religious claims. To avoid the opposition between faith and reason by saying they are *both* right is as unproductive as maintaining that only one of them is right. Surely there must be a better way!

Part Two

SHIFTING THE AXIS

5

THE FABRIC
OF EXPERIENCE

The aim of Part Two is to relocate the axis around which the central concepts of experience, meaning, and knowledge revolve, by way of establishing a post-critical philosophy, one that is more conducive to the philosophy of religion. My broader contention is that the following perspective on these three pivotal concepts not only is helpful to constructing a more fruitful religious philosophy but that it provides a more cogent understanding of human existence as well. The fulcrum for this fresh angle of approach will be the insights of Maurice Merleau-Ponty, Ludwig Wittgenstein, and Michael Polanyi.

The present chapter, as well as the two immediately following it, will constitute an invitation to consider the notions of experience, meaning, and knowledge in the light of a set of root metaphors quite distinct from those which guide the critical posture as outlined in Part One. To oversimplify by way of introduction, the root metaphors of critical philosophy are primarily those of vision and abstract thought, while those of a post-critical philosophy are more tactile and kinesthetic in character. The former emphasize distance, staticity, passivity, and analysis, while the latter stress involvement, activity, and integration.[1]

Experience as Relational

The two traditional models of experience within Western thought are reductionism and dualism. Empiricism tends to be reductionistic and rationalism leans toward dualism. Both of these models lead to difficulties which result in an impasse between fact and value, between the objective and the subjective aspects of human experience. Thus if this impasse, or dichotomy, is to be overcome, the particular difficulties of these two models must be avoided. A brief but specific noting of these difficulties is in order before we move ahead to a fresh and more fruitful model.

In addition to the fact that *empiricist reductionism* treats experience too atomistically and ignores its directional or intentional characteristics, there is one major problem which causes it to fail as an account of the structure of experienced reality. At bottom this approach is based on the concept of *sensory association* as that which provides the unity of objects, persons, and events in our experience. The data come associated or "packaged" in certain patterns and we "construct" or infer entities on the basis of these patterns of association. The problem with this explanation of the unity of our experience is that it presupposes what it is supposed to explain. For the association of common sensory patterns entails a *recognition* of the common features being associated, and such recognition involves the active participation of the knower. Impressions printed on a blank tablet are and remain isolated data, never becoming unified wholes apart from the activity of a prehender.[2]

Rationalistic dualism, on the other hand, overplays the intellectual aspect of human experience. By defining experience and knowing as strictly a function of the powers and categories of the mind, it ends up stressing the role of *interpretation* to the exclusion of sensory factors. The chief problem here is how to explain the *lack of* and the *search for* knowledge, since if it is a function of the formative action of the mind, there should never be a shortage of knowledge. Ignorance and discovery, to say nothing of error, thus become the stumbling blocks of an overly intellectual account of human experience. To turn this objection around, if experienced reality is primarily a result of the workings of the human mind, it would seem that our claims to knowledge would generally be incorrigible. Since they are not, there must be something missing from the intellectualist account.[3]

Instead of trying to *describe* the structure of experience from the outside, it is herein submitted that it is more fruitful to seek to *display* it while and through engaging in it. An obviously vital and common aspect of human experience is the business of seeking to understand something, as we are presently attempting to do. In this activity we direct our attention toward that which we deem meaningful or understandable. In fact, it is safe to say that nearly all human activity and experience is characterized by this orientation toward meaning. The world is experienced *as* meaningful. We find ourselves *engaged* in meaningful activity, whether physical or mental, and we experience reality in terms of this meaning.

Thus things, persons, ideas, and events are experienced as "that with which we have to do"; they take on their reality in and through our meaningful interaction with them. They neither exist nor are known exclusively in and of themselves, nor as functions of our intellectual capacities. They are *encountered* in relationship, in the push and pull of everyday life. They can neither be ignored nor studied from a distance, for to do either is to engage in some sort of relationship with them. They are neither completely dependent on, nor completely independent of, us.

Another way of putting this is in terms of wholes and parts. We experience the world as constituted of meaningful wholes, as objects, persons, events, ideas, etc. Although by means of analysis we often can identify and scrutinize the particulars which comprise these comprehensive entities, it remains the case that we experience them, *engage* them, as unified wholes at the primordial or initial level. Thus any form of atomistic analysis, no matter how helpful, is an abstraction. In fact, the very act of identifying the particulars comprising a given whole is logically dependent on a recognition of them as parts of *that* specific whole. Analysis is therefore parasitic on holistic awareness.[4]

Experience can be said to have a *vectorial* or directional ($\longrightarrow$) structure according to which both the awareness dimension and the activity dimension of our existence are patterned. Our awareness has a *from-to* structure in that we are always and only aware of particulars, they only take on meaning, in relation to broader wholes which have already been endowed with meaning. Our active involvement, in like fashion, follows a from-to pattern. We move toward the entities constituting our world out of our own awareness of embodied personhood. Our world is experienced in relation to, in and through, our active engagement of it. This is what phenomenologists call "intentionality."

It is true, of course, that we must have initial exposure to the particulars comprising the wholes which constitute our experienced reality. But the gap between simple exposure to parts and meaningful experience of unified wholes is bridged neither by further exposure, as with empiricism, nor by the powers of the mind, as with rationalism. Rather, the gap is bridged by means of active *engagement and interaction* between the knowing subject and the particulars. Through such active encounter the prehender, who is a meaning-seeking being, comes to an integrative discernment of the unified wholes comprising experienced reality.[5]

The infant's awareness of its mother's face as the face of its mother is not innate, nor is it the result of simple empirical build-up. It is, rather, the result of the interactive relationship between the mother and the infant by means of touch and speech. The particulars of the face become a meaningful whole in and through the give-and-take of the mother-infant relationship.[6] The same integrative discernment characterizes other aspects of experienced reality. Learning to drive a stick-shift car is another excellent example. The integration of the particular movements comprising the process of driving—clutching, shifting, accelerating, and steering—are first experienced as wholes in and of themselves. They are related to as such from the standpoint of one's unified and embodied selfhood. But through imitation and practice these movements *become* the single, unified entity known as driving—they are then experienced as a single whole and no longer as distinct entities in and of themselves.

EXPERIENCE AS EMBODIED

Yet another crucial dimension of human experience is its embodied character. We are so "close to" ourselves in our bodies that we generally fail to appreciate the degree to which our entire existence is conditioned by our embodiment. In all situations there are varying ways or modes of participation. For example, in the card game of bridge one partner takes an active mode, while the other takes a passive mode. Or, in conversations one person often participates as the questioner and another as the answerer. At this present moment, I am functioning as a writer and you are functioning as a reader. Building on this notion of mode of being, it is helpful to point out that embodied existence is our way or mode of "being-in-the-world." Being a body defines the nature and structure of our experience.

The fundamental and primordial character of our embodiment is all the more striking when we recall that by and large philosophers in both the East and the West, and especially critical philosophers of the modern era, have conducted their business as if bodies are at best a necessary but unfortunate intruder and at worst do not exist at all. A post-critical philosophy, however, takes the constitutive character of embodiment as central to the development of an integrative understanding of human experience.

A helpful way to characterize this important feature of our existence is to think of our body as the *axis* of our experience. The world, in all of its multitudinous variety, comes to us in terms of our physical position and posture. The universe "curves," as it were, around our physicality; its entities "orbit" around us and not vice versa. This foundational fact is poignantly reflected in the grammar or logic of the term "here." Because it has no permanent referent, the term is difficult for children to learn to employ. "Here" is a function of the physical location of the speaker, it moves as it were with him or her, it defines the center of the individual's world. Even high-level abstractions, daydreaming, and the like are tethered to and thus are understood in terms of their relation to embodiment, since they take place within, are framed by, space and time experienced bodily.

A related way of bringing out the essential quality of our embodied existence is in terms of the notion of *fulcrum*. Not only does our world come to us as revolving around us, but we encounter and/or engage it in and through our bodies as the pivot or leverage point of the activity dimension of our existence. Our bodies serve as the juncture at which we interact with and affect the world. We move toward and into our world through our bodies, just as it moves toward and engages us through our bodies. For the obvious but nonetheless amazing fact is that our bodies are *both* us *and* part of the world. Our existence is constituted by them and their existence is constituted by the world.

The cruciality of this embodied character of our experience renders problematic traditional philosophic ideas of experience. As has been pointed out, dualistic rationalists tend to speak of human existence as essentially mental persons—of persons *being* minds and *having* bodies. Reductionistic empiricists, on the other hand, tend to analyze experience exclusively in terms of sensations, which in the final analysis reduce to mental phenomena. Neither approach acknowledges the central role played by the body in human experience, both in terms of knowledge and in terms of reality and/or being. Thus neither approach can begin to do justice to the vectorial quality of human experience, the way in which it is all structured by and around the prehender's place and orientation.

A corollary of the above theme is that of the centrality of *movement*.[7] It is not enough to stress the importance of embodiment to ascertaining the character of experience. One must also emphasize that this embodiment is active. It is through movement that we give expression to and come to know our embodiment. Through physical movement we come to indwell space and time, through physical movement we encounter other physical objects and come to understand extension and solidity. In a word, we interact with, or engage, our world because we exist *in* and move *through* it. It is truly surprising to reflect on how devoid of such notions modern philosophical accounts of experience, including those of Kant and especially those of contemporary analysts, are. Their dominant motif is one of static and passive observation and reception, whereas a moment's reflection on reflection itself clearly reveals the primordial character of embodied activity and exploration.

A dramatic rendition of the embodiment motif within human life is made available in the work of Jean Piaget.[8] He has established that children exhibit reasoning ability before they become full members of the linguistic community. He concludes from this that we think before, and thus independently of, speaking. What often goes unnoticed, however, is that the reasoning and thinking involved is not the sort of conscious awareness and progression we usually associate with such terms. Rather, it is a rational ability exhibited in the child's *physical activity*. Locating an object that has been covered up, first by a hat and then by a scarf, does not stand for or represent a mentalistic kind of thought or reasoning process—it *is* a reasoning process embodied in physical activity.

In like manner, when we acquire skills and thus can be said to know how to do such and such, to have a knowledge of it, it is clear that this knowledge is somehow *in our bodies*. Thus it is proper to say that often we think in, with, and through our bodies. Very complex skills—such as riding a bicycle and swimming which, once learned, can hardly ever be completely lost and which at the same time cannot be explained or passed on by formula—illustrate the degree to which we think with our bodies. In fact, it is possible to argue that the basis for all knowledge is to be found in such skills—think of maintaining our balance, grasping tools, speaking—but more of this in Chapter 7.

EXPERIENCE AS SYNAESTHETIC

Another feature of the account of experience given by critical philosophy, one that renders it self-defeating, is that it deals with each of the senses comprising experience independently of the others. This is a natural extension of the atomistic posture. In point of fact, however, human experience is *synaesthetic* in quality; our world is experienced as a total fabric woven together out of inextricable sensory threads. Vision, hearing, and touch almost always come simultaneously, each affecting and interpreting the other. Our experience is of the whole which they create, not of them as individual sensory media, nor of their individual data. Thus whatever account we give of experience not only must take this synesthetic motif into consideration but must *begin* with and from it.

This leads directly to a broader point. As was noted in section 1 of the present chapter, experience is essentially *relational*. Thus it is helpful in general to approach an understanding of it from the perspective provided by a *field* or *fabric* root metaphor, rather than an atomistic or individualistic one. Such an approach not only allows one to deal with the different aspects of experience as whole rather than as isolated particulars but it provides as well a holistic vantage point for relating to the comprehensive character of the total, environmental quality of experience. Human experience is helpfully understood in analogue with electromagnetic and gravitational force fields, wherein the elements comprising the whole are better defined in terms of the dynamics of the field than in terms of individual particulars.

Another related root metaphor that provides a useful handle for grasping the holistic character of experience is that of the *gearing* mechanism of a complex machine. In such a machine the individual wheels may be identified and scrutinized as separate parts, but their essential nature can be understood only in terms of their functional relation to the whole. Each part is endowed with meaning, and in the deepest sense with being, as and in a relationship to the other parts. The machine as a whole is more or other than simply a *sum* of the individual parts. Moreover, the cogs of the individual wheels *mesh* with and *gear* into each other in such a way as to make it clear that the definition of the machine can really be given only in terms of the dynamics of the integrated and symbiotic quality of this cogging relationship.

When this way of approaching the nature of experience is applied to epistemological issues some interesting and important considerations come to light. The standard way of working with the nature of knowledge is by defining it in terms of a relationship between the knower and the known, albeit a static and distant sort of relationship. Whether one speaks of knowledge as correspondence or coherence, the overall effect is that of a snapshot which isolates a belief and a state of affairs in order to compare them. The knower is pictured as holding certain beliefs and the known is thought of as the objective *given* of experience—and the two exist side by side, connected only by this logical or structural, but basically optional or accidental, parallel. The knower and the known are defined in and of themselves and not in terms of one another.

When, however, the basic epistemological situation is approached from

dimension is experienced *in and through* a less rich dimension. An ontological hierarchy can be constructed beginning with the physical or material dimension of experience as the least complex, moving on up through the social, moral, and aesthetic dimensions, and culminating with the religious dimension as the richest, most comprehensive.

Consider the following example. Four persons standing on a bridge overlooking a river witness a small child fall into the water. The first gives a complete account of the physical dimension of the event in terms of height, weight, angle, depth, etc. The second person's account differs from that of the first, not by denying anything said or affirming that anything was left out, but rather by calling attention to the aesthetic dimension as mediated by the arrangement of the physical particulars comprising the event. The aesthetic is experienced in and through the physical. Of course the shallowness and abnormality of both of these accounts is highlighted by that of the third person, who does not contradict either of them but affirms a discernment of the moral dimension in the situation by acknowledging their obligation to respond to the child in need. Moral awareness is richer than and thus mediated through the other forms of awareness.

The account of the fourth person may differ from all three of the previous ones, once again not by disagreeing with anything in them but by giving witness to yet another dimension disclosed in and through the situation. In addition to experiencing the physical, aesthetic, moral, and whatever other dimensions of reality there might be, the religious person claims to be interacting with a more complex, richer, and more comprehensive dimension than any of them in this and every situation—not distinct from them, but *in and through* them. The religious dimension transcends the others by providing the hinge by means of which they are integrated and endowed with deeper meaning. Because of the mediated structure of the dimensional hierarchy, however, the religious dimension of experience is not discerned over and above the other dimensions. They provide the juncture or context for religious awareness, and thus their particular shape and form are of decisive importance for it. I shall deal with this whole question in more detail in Chapter 9.

6

MEANING
IN CONTEXT

One of the chief shortcomings of the critical approach to philosophy in general and to philosophy of religion in particular is a narrow concept of meaning. Not only is the notion of meaning generally equated with linguistic meaning, but the definition of the latter is usually confined to the picture theory of meaning as well. The consequences of such an approach for both the philosophy of language and the nature of religious language are as negative as they are obvious. It is the aim of this chapter to present an understanding of meaning which is at once more broad and more fruitful than that offered by critical philosophy. The pivotal idea in this presentation is the overriding contextual character of meaning, both in its linguistic and in its nonlinguistic dimensions.

Reality Linguistically Constituted

An issue often debated concerns the extent to which the structure of our particular natural language determines the character and shape of the world we experience. This debate frequently broadens into a discussion of the extent to which reality is a function of language and/or thought in general. At one extreme stand those who maintain that reality is what it is, with language simply serving as one way of responding to it. At the other extreme are those who contend that the only reality we can talk and think about is that which is constructed for us by the structure of our language. In between are a wide variety of positions that seek to trace the connection between language and reality according to a more complex pattern.

One way to avoid the difficulties attendant to the above extremes—namely, naiveté and complete relativism respectively—is to assert that experienced reality is *linguistically constituted*. This way of speaking acknowledges the crucial role played by language in forming our world, thereby avoiding naiveté, while at the same time leaving room for other constitutive factors as well, thus transcending "hard-nosed" relativism.[1] We are not in a position to compare our linguistically experienced world with the world as it is unexperienced by us. Nonetheless, within the world provided by our language we find it helpful and even necessary to distinguish more comprehensive and fruitful propositions and perspectives from those which are less so—and we make these moves in and through language as well. Thus even though we cannot transcend language, we are not entirely bound by it either. It *participates* in the constitution of our world without necessarily determining its character entirely.

The suggestion here is that we view language as the relationship between our experienced world and reality as it would be apart from our interaction with it. Language functions as the thread out of which the fabric comprising our world is woven, and our activity—both linguistic and nonlinguistic—constitutes the moves whereby this fabric is woven. In such a relational understanding of the role of language the emphasis is on the logical priority of the interactive relationship itself as constitutive of the poles—much as an electromagnetic field creates its positive and negative poles—rather than being on the poles themselves as self-contained entities which then enter into relationship. To return to the weaving metaphor, the edges which define and limit the fabric are themselves created *by* the fabric as it grows out of the interactive process of weaving.

Traditionally we tend to think of social reality as embodied in language and culture, as secondary to and superimposed upon the physical world, as both arbitrary and optional. The suggestion being made here is that social reality is every bit as "natural" and primordial as its physical counterpart. We are born into a world comprised of both a physical and a social dimension. Both of these dimensions are mediated to us, we interact with both of them, in and through language. If we did not participate in language, the world would be a distinctly different place, for although physical objects and relationships might be said to remain pretty much the same, our experience of them would not. For example, doorknobs and handles, in some sense, *exist* for dogs, but they are not experienced *as,* and thus do *not* exist *as,* doorknobs and handles in the functional sense for them.

The cruciality of language to the shape and structure of experienced reality can perhaps be put in the following way. We wake up, as it were, or find ourselves participating in language, when and as we ask the question about the relationship between language and reality—we are already embarked on or committed to language long before such questions come up. In fact, it is only *because* we participate in linguistic activity that we ever raise questions about its nature and function—and thus in a deep sense we already know what it is and how it works. In this way we can see that reality is linguistically constituted, for our very asking of the question about the relationship between language and the world clearly displays and embodies that relationship. Language is as fundamental to our intellectual life, no matter how broadly or narrowly conceived, as breathing is to our physical life.[2]

To turn our attention to the other pole of this symbiotic relationship, it is helpful to remind ourselves that not only does our world come into being in and through language but we ourselves become human beings in the full (not just the biological) sense by means of linguistic activity as well. Language is definitive of our "form of life," to use Wittgenstein's term, or of our way of "being-in-the-world," to use Merleau-Ponty's. An amazing anthropological fact is that *all* peoples, no matter how "primitive" or ancient, have highly developed and complex linguistic systems. We have a tendency to imagine that preliterate, technologically simple people have simple, primitive languages. However, even the aborigines in the outback of Australia, who spend most of their waking hours searching for roots to eat, have a highly complex linguistic system. There simply is no such thing as a "primitive" natural language.

The definitive character of linguistic activity vis-à-vis being human is dramatically punctuated by Helen Keller's account of her transition from a prelingual being to a member of the speaking community. She describes her early childhood as a kind of "phantom" existence wherein she never performed an "intentional" act, but merely responded to physical stimuli in a sort of push-pull world. It was through being spoken to in tactile sign language that she entered into reciprocal relationships with both human beings and the physical world.[3] The studies of wolf children or feral children who are reared outside of the linguistic dimension reinforce this point as well. The difference is not simply one between humans who speak and humans who do not speak. It is, rather, the difference between being human in actuality and being human in potentiality.

One major reason why we tend to think of language as an optional or secondary aspect of both human life and the world is that we treat it as exclusively a phenomenon of the mind. In part this is due to our preoccupation with the written as distinguished from the spoken word. It seems clear, however, that the former is entirely dependent on the latter, and that the latter is inextricably bound up with the *embodied* character of our existence. Not only is speech produced and received by means of physical apparati, but it takes place within a somatic milieu of facial expressions, bodily gestures, and physical postures. The proverbial joke about people not being able to talk if their hands were tied behind their backs points up an important truth.

We not only interpret physical activity on the basis of accompanying speech, but we often interpret the spoken word in terms of the bodily movements that accompany it. Thus not only is language inextricably bound up with specific gestures and facial expressions, it is part and parcel of our total behavioral existence. Our motivations and intentions are revealed in the dynamic give-and-take between our deeds and our words. The meaning of our actions and utterances, as well as the meaning of our lives, is a function of the reciprocal interaction between them. Here again we can see that our world is linguistically constituted.

LANGUAGE AS SOCIAL ACTIVITY

The foregoing remarks lead right into a second major feature of the linguistic dimension of human existence, one that is crucial to a post-critical understanding. Although it often goes unnoticed, it should be obvious that language is something people *do*. Language does not exist in and of itself, independently of human beings, but rather exists *between* speaking persons. This point is reflected in the fact that anthropologists frequently and insightfully refer to language as the first and most important *tool* invented by humankind.[4] People speak in the context of their physical and social environment in order to accomplish certain tasks—speaking, in short, is a human *activity*.

Within this framework linguistic meaning is best understood as a function of *use in context*.[5] The difficulty with the picture theory of meaning, as developed by critical philosophy and presented in Chapter 2, is not that language is never used to picture states of affairs, but that such uses were set up as the only legitimate standard of meaningfulness. This narrow conception of meaning simply fails to do any kind of justice to the vast complexity and richness of linguistic activity, whether on the ordinary or the theoretic level. In point of fact, the statement of the picture theory of meaning is itself a use of language which does not conform to the criterion that it proposes, since it functions as a proposal or rule of operation rather than as a picture of anything.

The vast array of uses to which linguistic expression is put demands a broader, more flexible understanding of meaning. In speaking we do everything from performing ritualistic deeds (such as greetings) through wondering and speculating to joking, confessing, praying, and deciding. The fact that the list of activities accomplished through speech is essentially endless (it even includes the making of lists) suggests what some have called the "open-textured" character of language. Not only is language a sort of rough-and-ready kind of phenomenon, in the sense that its various forms and uses crisscross and overlap in surprising yet effective ways, but language itself is never complete.

By this I mean not only that new uses and expressions are being added while others are being discarded in a continual process, but that although at any given time and place every language contains a very limited number of constituents and rules, whatever *needs* to be said *can* come to be said in any language. The language can be formed to fit the situation, to meet the need. In fact, the notion of completeness has no more place in relation to language than it does in relation to the streets of a city or a system of numbers—new connections can always be forged.

The focusing of meaning in terms of use gives rise to the importance of *context* as a mediator of meaning. Linguistic utterances do not occur in a vacuum, but rather take place in concrete situations between specific people for fairly well defined reasons. The physical setting, the previous utterances, the roles of the persons involved all comprise the context or the parameters within which communication transpires. Thus it is not only important but necessary that one be aware—whether focally or subsidiarily—of such aspects of the linguistic event when seeking to interpret it. "March," when said by a drill leader on the parade ground, has a very different meaning from "March" when said in response to the question, "What month is this?" Examples of this type could be multiplied endlessly.

Another aspect of linguistic context is that of *conventions*. Certain words and/or ways of speaking have come to be used in standardized ways and this standardization is important in the conveyance of meaning. "How are you?" or "What's happenin'?" are conventional greetings and not requests for detailed accounts. We learn to distinguish between utterances, such as those on road signs, which are commands ("Stop," "Yield," etc.), and those which are invitations ("Buy Gas Here," "Have a Drink," etc.). Gestures and facial expressions also become conventionalized and serve to mediate the meaning of various remarks. Think of the many different inflections, movements, and eyeball effects that can accompany the simple utterance, "Really!"

Overriding all of the above, or rather connecting and guiding it all, are the *intentions* or purposes which the speaker seeks to realize in, through, and by speaking in the way she or he does. This pragmatic dimension of language is the *raison d'être* of the syntactic and semantic dimensions. People do not simply speak, or even give descriptions or name items, as an end in itself. Rather, they do these things with certain ends in mind, with certain tasks to get done. To attempt to analyze meaning apart from context, convention, and intentions, as critical philosophers generally do, will inevitably distort both the meaning of a given utterance and one's understanding of meaning in general. The abstract analysis and trivial examples employed in critical philosophy both reflect and contribute to the shallow character of such an approach to language.[6]

One final feature of viewing language as a social activity warrants discussion. The commonality of certain tasks and the pervasive character of conventions, together with the communal nature of human existence, give rise to what Wittgenstein termed specific "language games" within the broader fabric of language in general. Certain areas of human experience cluster together, developing loosely patterned ways of speaking and acting. When we learn our way into these language games or patterns, the meaning of our utterances within them is in large part a function of the conventions and customs constituting them. This meaning is essentially a *group phenomenon,* since it arises in a speaking community which shares a common experience and life pattern. The traditional disciplines, such as art, science, philosophy, and history, as well as various dimensions of popular culture, such as sports, entertainment, advertising, and politics, serve as excellent examples of communities that could be said to participate in language games indigenous to their common experiences.

A final point of clarification. It is important to bear in mind that in no cases are the language games entirely separate and distinct from one another. There are no hard-and-fast, no well-defined lines of demarcation among them. Rather, language games fade into and overlap with each other in a fascinating and sometimes madding fashion. In point of fact, they grow out of each other in an organic way, each seemingly new one parasiting on others both while it is being formed and as it continues to function. Thus no language game is self-justifying or autonomous, even though each develops unique patterns of its own. To say "This language game is played" does not imply that each language game is self-contained and bears no relationship to others. For each one that *is* played is played within a broader fabric of both linguistic and nonlinguistic behavior and gets its life in part from that fabric.

This is an especially important point to keep clear with respect to religious language. There is a rather common misunderstanding that Wittgenstein's notion of language games lends support to the view that religious language is *sui generis,* a view often termed "Wittgensteinian fideism."[7] But clearly, not only is such a position out of line with the way in which language games develop and function (religious language included) but it is based on a misreading of the insights of Wittgenstein. He nowhere implies such autonomy and expressly speaks of the overlapping and crisscrossing character of linguistic "neighborhoods." We speak of God and faith within and out of our common experience and in ways that connect with other dimensions of life and language. More on this in Chapter 10.

THE PRINCIPLE OF SUFFICIENT PRECISION

Part of the legacy of critical philosophy is the presupposition that meaning is directly correlated with precision. The often unstated, though sometimes articulated, assumption is that unless a term or statement is precisely defined and/or analyzed, its meaning is essentially unclear. We have been taught to believe that ambiguity and vagueness are stumbling blocks to meaningful communication and that the closer we can get to absolute precision the better. In fact, critical philosophers often maintain that actual understanding of meaning obtains only when absolute precision is attained. This was the contention behind Russell and Whitehead's efforts in *Principia Mathematica* and Rudolf Carnap's development of artificial or "ideal" languages.

The vision of absolute precision generally involves the idea that if each term in a language can be assigned a strictly specific meaning, definable either by means of other precisely defined terms or by means of simple ostensive pointing to the object or quality in question, then all ambiguity and vagueness would be eliminated. Even if it is begrudgingly acknowledged that such complete precision is impossible, because of the limitations inherent in human memory, time and space, etc., it is nonetheless argued that it is always best to get as close to this ideal as possible. The greater the precision, the better the communication. Some would even go so far as to contend that unless certain *basic* terms and propositions are defined precisely, no meaningful communication can transpire.

Now, against this general position I want to argue that absolute precision is neither possible, nor necessary, nor always desirable. Beginning with the last point, it should be clear that from a pragmatic perspective there are situations in which diplomacy and/or tact would render it advisable to make our utterances deliberately vague or ambiguous. Moreover, in certain exploratory and educational contexts we must be careful not to box ourselves in with overly precise terminology lest we obscure or even exclude the very possibilities we are seeking to engender or discover.[8]

In addition to the above considerations, it must also be pointed out that absolute precision is impossible. First, there is no definition that can be given of any term or statement which qualifies as *absolutely* precise. No matter what terms are employed, each of them in turn must be given a precise definition of its own in order for the initial definition to be precise—and each term of these ensuing definitions must be given a precise definition as well, *ad infinitum.* Thus if absolute precision is a requirement for meaningfulness, no one would ever be able to communicate at all. Indeed, even the above sentence could not be understood, since all the terms in it have not been previously defined. The difficulty involved here is sometimes known as the "I can't get started with you" problem, since the required beginning point in communicating is systematically elusive.

One way of avoiding this infinite regress is by becoming as absolutely precise as possible, specifically in terms of mathematical and logical symbolism, within the confines of a highly abstract context while leaving the terms that comprise this context undefined. This gives the illusion of complete precision, but in reality only avoids the problem by setting up an arbitrary cutoff point. Moreover, the price paid for such conceptual rigor and precision is irrelevance and/or untranslatability, since the point of connection between the terms within the abstract context and those of ordinary language is left undefined. To put the point somewhat differently, the fundamental difficulty with the notion of an ideal language, even within a small context, is that it still has to be constructed out of, explained in terms of, and learned from within the rough-and-ready, imprecise texture of ordinary natural languages. As Wittgenstein so poignantly put it:

> The more narrowly we examine actual language, the sharper becomes the conflict between it and our requirement. (For the crystalline purity of logic was, of course, not a result of investigation: it was a requirement.) The conflict becomes intolerable; the requirement is now in danger of becoming empty.—We have got on to slippery ice where there is no friction and so in a certain sense the conditions are ideal, but also, just because of that, we are unable to walk. We want to walk; so we need friction. Back to the rough ground![9]

Another way of avoiding the infinite regress difficulty, it is sometimes suggested, is by grounding verbal definitions finally in nonverbal, ostensive definitions. Pointing to an object or a quality while saying its name is thought to provide a precise foundation for the verbal definitions and precision of concepts based thereon. The reason this tack will not work is that pointing is itself an extremely imprecise phenomenon. Not only must one have a great deal of practice and understanding to be able to "read" a pointing finger or an arrow, as anyone who has ever worked with dogs and small children will attest, but pointing is itself a concept that cannot be defined with precision. In fact, in order to comprehend that pointing to an object or a quality, overlooking for the moment that objects and qualities can hardly be singled out with precision by something as crude as a pointing finger, while uttering certain words constitutes *defining* those words, we already have to know what definitions are in some sense. In other words, how do we come to know that pointing to something while saying its name *means* that this particular word is the name of this object (or class of objects)? And so either the infinite regress continues or it is brought to an end arbitrarily. In either case, absolute precision has not been achieved.

Having shown that the ideal of complete precision is impossible, we now need to establish that it is unnecessary. In spite of the failure of critical philosophy to make precision a defining characteristic of meaningfulness, the fact remains that people communicate quite well. In fact, even the efforts to establish the critiques of absolute precision as an ideal are themselves understood quite apart from their key terms being defined with precision. The so-called vagaries and ambiguities of ordinary language are sufficient, both for the tasks of everyday life and for the construction of specialized language games wherein increased precision is required. We speak in a rough-and-ready way to accomplish certain tasks within social contexts and out of shared experience. When a task calls for more precision we devise ways of making our language more precise. The criterion for determining meaningfulness is not absolute precision, but whatever degree of precision enables us to accomplish the task at hand. The criterion is *significant precision.*[10]

To put the point slightly differently, we speak within a roughly defined range of precision that is appropriate to everyday life until real or anticipated difficulties arise. Then we construct more circumspect ways of speaking, either for the moment, as when negotiating with a neighbor, or so as to be codified into a system of rules, as when establishing laws governing the sale of property, etc. Or we may devise a specialized language game for carrying on various scientific activities, such as in the case of chemistry or calculus. What is important to see in all this is that it is the more precise ways of speaking that are parasitic on the less precise, and not the other way around. We must understand the meaning of a term in some sense before we can make it more precise. To quote Wittgenstein again:

> To repeat, we can draw a boundary—for a special purpose. Does it take that to make the concept usable? Not at all! (Except for that special purpose.) No more than it took the definition: 1 pace = 75 cm. to make the measure of length "one pace" usable. And if you want to say "But still, before that it wasn't an exact measure," then I reply: very well, it was an inexact one.—Though you still owe me a definition of exactness.
>
> "But if the concept 'game' is uncircumscribed like that, you don't really know what you mean by a 'game.' "—When I give the description: "The ground was quite covered with plants"—do you want to say I don't know what I am talking about until I can give a definition of a plant?[11]

THE PRIMACY OF METAPHOR

According to the dictates of critical thought, metaphoric uses of language are *merely* creative ways of making statements that can be made more meaningfully in a cognitive sense quite apart from metaphor. In the words of Paul Edwards, "There are two types of metaphor, those that can be translated into nonmetaphoric language and those that cannot. The former are cognitively significant and the latter are not."[12] The central thesis here is that precise language is logically prior to metaphoric language. This implies that metaphoric utterances arise only *after* meanings have been established nonmetaphorically or literally. For one must know what one means before one can devise metaphoric ways of expressing it.

The fact is, of course, that the critical account of the relationship between precision and metaphor is essentially backwards.[13] Not only is it contrary to its own "positivistic" posture, which emphasizes how far we have come in modern times by way of transcending the mythological and metaphorical vagaries of ancient and medieval times, but it is out of step with the way metaphoric language actually functions, both in everyday usage and in scientific enterprises. It is not the case that we first develop a set of precise notions and then cast about for a creative metaphor in which to express them. Rather, both our everyday and our specialized insights are frequently initially expressed in metaphors and/or models which later may or may not be refined and precised, depending on our needs. Speaking of Manhattan as a vast ant colony or of the DNA molecule as a double helix is not merely a figurative way of expressing a previously defined precise concept. It is, rather, the metaphoric matrix out of which further insights and more specialized ways of speaking arise.[14]

Thomas Kuhn[15] has developed this point in terms of the relationship between "paradigms" and "normal science" in which the former, functioning as pregnant models, provide the framework within which the latter, seeking precise answers to specific problems, is carried on. In any scientific era, such as the Newtonian or the Einsteinian, the basic models or root metaphors are not translated into precise logical and/or empirical language. Rather, they serve as the bedrock upon which further precising moves are worked out. Thus the clear-cut line between cognitive precision and noncognitive metaphor sought by critical philosophers cannot be drawn, because it does not exist. Cognitivity is a symbiotic dimension of meaning roughed out between the poles of metaphor and precision.

It is even possible to argue that the basic metaphoric categories through which we perceive and conceive our world in a sense determine the structure of that world. Many experiments in perception have shown that we tend to see and hear what we expect, either because of what we believe or are told we will experience.[16] On the conceptual level we can all remember how our understanding of the world changed when we were introduced to such ideas as role-playing and game theory. In effect, the very constitution of reality is altered when such concepts are employed. To call a person a "nigger" consistently is to create a nigger, in the same way as to relate to a person as a friend tends to create a friend. This constitutive power of language in relation to reality has been termed "the Orphic voice" because it brings the world into existence even as did the singing of Orpheus.[17]

The overall point of this chapter has been to stress the way in which the context surrounding a linguistic event mediates its meaning. Contextually mediated meaning stands in direct contrast to the ideal of absolute precision as propounded by critical philosophy because it relies upon the more flexible notion of significant or sufficient precision. In addition, this understanding of linguistic meaning dovetails appropriately with the construing of experienced reality in terms of a hierarchy of mediated dimensions. For the language we use to communicate our awareness of mediated dimensions of reality ought itself to have a mediated structure. Thus the key concept of mediation serves to alter the critical understanding of both experience and meaning in a way that makes them richer and more flexible.

7

KNOWLEDGE
THROUGH PARTICIPATION

The focal point of the critical approach to epistemology is the cruciality of the concept of inference. All knowledge claims must be based on a clearly defined inferential process, whether deductive or inductive, in order to qualify as bona fide knowledge. The particulars of this approach were spelled out in Chapter 3. It is now time, against the background of the two immediately preceding chapters, to give attention to a fresh placing of the epistemological axis within a *post*-critical philosophy. The main theme of this endeavor will be the relationship between knowledge and participation.

Knowing as an Activity

An important feature of the critical understanding of knowledge is its essentially passive character. To oversimplify, according to this view knowledge is something that happens to, or occurs within, the knowing subject as a result of exposure to or observation of experience. To put it slightly differently, knowledge is defined by critical philosophers as an essentially static relationship between the knower's mind and the outside world. A post-critical understanding of knowing begins by acknowledging (1) that there is no knowledge apart from active engagement between the knowing subject and that which is known and (2) that knowing itself is a kind of *doing*, that knowledge is not *had* as much as it is *done*. In both of these respects participation plays a crucial role.

Put bluntly, it is important to bear in mind that knowing is something *persons* do, that there is no knowledge apart from knowers, even as there is no language apart from speakers. Moreover, knowing always takes place within a concrete historical and social context. We come to knowledge as a result of our participation in the lives and thoughts of other persons both past and present. Knowledge is held, discovered, and experienced jointly on the basis of mutual exploration, support, and communication. Persons act in the world, and in so doing they both acquire and exhibit knowledge.

The cruciality of activity and participation to the knowing process is dramatically illustrated by the all-important role of *movement* in the learning of infants. If an infant is not allowed to move around and interact with its environment through its body in three-dimensional space, it will not come to a knowledge of the world at all. Piaget's studies have highlighted the fact that very young children develop and display cognitive abilities by means of their physical behavior prior to doing so by means of their linguistic behavior. Learning to crawl and learning to turn the head to the right in anticipation of the reappearance of a face that has moved around behind it to the left are cognitive deeds of which it is proper and insightful to say that knowing and doing are inextricably bound up together.

Another way of bringing out the activity or the participatory character of knowing is by means of the contrast between the inferential process and what is helpfully termed an *"integrative act."*[1] In the former case the knower moves from isolated particulars, be they data or premises, to a comprehensive conclusion by means of a process that is reversible, in the sense that the steps can be identified and retraced. In the latter case, however, the gap between one's initial encounter with isolated particulars and the grasp of the comprehensive whole is bridged not by a reversible, step-by-step process but by an irreversible act of integration. The individual particulars come to be experienced as comprising a meaningful entity as a result of the interaction between them and the knower's embodied and active mind. It is the engagement of the particulars by the mind which enables the knowing subject to understand the whole, and once it is understood one cannot return to the original state of ignorance again.

What is of paramount epistemological significance is that the notion of integrative act is logically prior to that of inference. As Aristotle pointed out, all deductive knowing is dependent on inductive knowing (for premises with which to begin) *and* all inductive knowing in turn is dependent on a prior act of recognition which provides the context within which it is possible to experience and acknowledge the data and/or the premises in question *as such.* In other words, apart from an initial integrative act, which places the knower on "square one" epistemologically speaking, there would be no inferential movement from square one to squares two, three, etc. Moreover, since all inferential knowing must begin from square one, the initial move from zero to square one cannot be based in inference at all.

The dynamics of the integrative act are grounded in active participation. The knower becomes a knower by exploration and interaction, the particulars and/or the data are experienced in the push and pull of living as we relate to our physical, social, and conceptual environment. We encounter objects, the ground, pressures, distances, and the like, coming to terms with them when and as we engage and are engaged by them. They are *experienced as* the realities we know them as *because* we interact with them, not the other way around. The same holds true for our knowledge of persons. Out of our involvement with mother, father, sister, grandfather, and strangers arises our knowledge of them—they are constituted by the relationship we have with them and by the meaning they bear for us.

The general ignoring and frequent denying of the centrality of active participation to the process and definition of knowing has led to what might be termed "the cult of objectivity." The goal of critical philosophy is to eliminate the involvement of the knowing subject from the definition of what constitutes knowledge in order to ensure the closest possible approximation to an absolutely "pure" conception. The contention is that only that which is purged of all "subjective" elements can qualify as genuine knowledge. The basic difficulty with this goal is threefold. First, it is utopian and thus engenders all sorts of confusion and frustration by being in principle unrealizable. Second, and more fundamental, it belies the obvious structure of the knowing process as outlined above. Third, it is internally inconsistent, since it is based on a valuing of objectivity which itself cannot meet the criterion of eliminating subjective features such as valuing.

It is at once more realistic, helpful, and consistent to acknowledge at the outset that all knowing takes place in, indeed is constituted by, *relationship*. To know means to interact with in the sense of acquiring knowledge *through* participation. To know means to interact with in the sense of exhibiting and embodying understanding *in* participation. Thus to know means to interact with in the sense of being defined *as* participation. Every knower, from the theoretic scientist interacting with abstract symbols to the skillful athlete judging the angle and speed of a ball, acquires and employs his or her knowledge in relational participation with that which is known. Thus, knowing is an activity, a doing.[2]

The Tacit Structure of Knowing

Perhaps the linchpin of the entire effort to construct a post-critical philosophy lies in the distinction (not "dichotomy") between explicit and tacit knowing. The critical approach to epistemology insists that all knowledge must be explicit or articulatable. The post-critical posture begins by acknowledging that, in the words of Michael Polanyi, "We know more than we can say" and that all explicit knowledge is grounded in unarticulated, tacit knowing. The nature and the ramifications of this distinction deserve unpacking. I propose to do this by means of explicating two more fundamental distinctions out of which the one between explicit and tacit knowledge arises.[3]

The first distinction that needs to be explicated is that between "focal" and "subsidiary" awareness. In any given cognitive context there are some factors of which the knowing subject is aware because he is directing his attention to them. Such awareness is termed "focal." In the same context there are also factors of which the knower is aware even though he is not focusing on them. This is termed "subsidiary" awareness. By way of example, in the context of reading or hearing my words the reader or the listener is focusing his attention on their meaning, not on the letters or phonemes of which they are comprised, nor even on the words themselves. Nevertheless, it is obvious that the reader is subsidiarily aware of both the letters or phonemes and the words.

It is clear that this distinction, like all contextual distinctions, is a relative one. In other words, a person can direct his attention to those factors of which formerly he was subsidiarily aware, thereby becoming focally aware of them. In like manner, one can become subsidiarily aware of those factors of which he was focally aware. This is obvious with respect to the above example of letters, words, and meaning. It also is true with respect to other levels of experience such as the physical, the psychological, and the moral. In all these cases the cognitive context is brought into being by the knowing subject "attending from" that of which he is subsidiarily aware and "attending to" that of which he is focally aware.

The major epistemological point to be drawn from this distinction is that not only is cognitive awareness an exclusive function of contextual significance, it is a function of a continuum between focal and subsidiary awareness as well. Thus knowledge as awareness simply cannot be limited to that of which we are focally aware. In order for there even to be a context in which one can be focally aware of some factors, there must also be some factors of which one is only subsidiarily aware. In short, one must have a "place to stand"—to attend from—in order to be able to attend to anything at all.

The second distinction is one between the two poles of what might be called "the activity continuum." All human activity can be placed on a scale somewhere between "conceptualization," which is most often verbal, and "embodiment," which pertains to nonverbal behavior. It should be obvious that the vast majority of human behavior is an inextricable mixture of both verbal and bodily activity. Even when one is simply thinking (to say nothing of talking), certain bodily activities can be detected as integral; and when one is simply engaged in bodily action, there are corresponding conceptual (and even verbal) efforts which are part of the activity. Abstract mathematicians and yoga meditators register brain waves and circulatory processes. Athletes talk to themselves or to their opponents, sailors and work crews sing as they work, and lovers feel it necessary to "whisper sweet nothings" to each other.

There is a sense in which every activity on this continuum can be said to involve the making of a judgment. In addition to assertions and thought processes, which obviously involve judgment-making, it can be shown that even such so-called noncognitive verbalizations as "Hello" and "Oh!" imply the making of a judgment concerning the situation in which they are uttered. Even exclamations have a "depth grammar." At the other end of the continuum, even such almost totally bodily behavior as a reflex action implies the making of a judgment about the situation in which it is performed. This is why we say that a ballplayer "misjudged" the ball or that a motorist "misjudged" the speed of the other car. Any given human act is performed within a context which renders it an act of judgment in relation to that context.

An important corollary to this "activity continuum" is that any human behavior, to the extent that it implies the making of a judgment, involves a knowledge claim. There are two sides of this corollary that need explanation. One side is that all activity, whether verbal or nonverbal, involves the actor in a knowledge claim and can be evaluated as either appropriate (true) or inappropriate (false). Thus there is no room for a hard-and-fast distinction between "saying" as a cognitive activity and "doing" as a noncognitive activity. Whether a particular act is verbal or nonverbal is always a question of degree, but there is no question of whether or not an act implies a cognitive judgment. To some extent all acts do!

The other side of this corollary is that all knowledge claims involve the commitment, or "personal backing," of the one making the claim. The point is simply that even though a knowledge claim is implicit in a given action, be it verbal or nonverbal, the person involved is nonetheless responsible for substantiating the claim. We hold people accountable for their reflex actions as well as for their verbal promises. All human activity is predicated upon the reality of responsible commitment.

Now I shall bring these two distinctions together. The first distinction was between focal and subsidiary awareness, and the second was between conceptual and bodily activity. When these two sets of distinctions are related to each other the result is yet a third distinction between explicit and tacit knowledge. The relationship can be visualized by imagining the "awareness continuum" and the "activity continuum" as dimensions that intersect each other. When the poles of focal awareness and conceptual activity are related the result is "explicit knowledge." When the poles of subsidiary awareness and bodily activity are related the result is "tacit knowledge." As every awareness and activity is a mixture of its respective poles, so every form of knowledge is a mixture of both explicit and tacit elements. In other words, relating the first two continua in this way produces yet a third continuum—the knowledge continuum—between the explicit and tacit poles.

To put this distinction another way, every context in which cognitive significance is present is comprised of both tacit and explicit factors. That is, the context exists somewhere on the continuum between these two poles. The interaction between those factors of which the subject is focally aware and the subject's conceptual response gives rise to explicit knowledge. Such is the case when one attends to and names an object in one's perceptual field. The interaction between those factors of which the subject is subsidiarily aware and his or her more nonverbal, bodily response gives rise to tacit knowledge. Such is the case when the person, attending to and naming an object in his or her perceptual field, is not conscious of but still must be said to know the functioning of the senses and discriminatory powers which render explicit knowledge possible. That the person knows these tacit factors can be made clear by being asked to focus on them, whereupon the person may become quite articulate about the movement of his or her head and hands and about the rational steps necessary in identifying an object. But then, some other factors will be supplying the tacit context within which this new focusing is taking place.

There are two further points about the relationship between explicit and tacit knowledge which need to be discussed by way of coming to a firmer understanding of the latter. Tacit knowledge not only is a legitimate form of knowledge but it is logically prior to explicit knowledge. In any situation the subject tacitly relies upon a large variety of factors in order to know any factors explicitly. Moreover, although what is known tacitly in one context may well be known explicitly in another context, some forms of tacit knowledge can never be known explicitly. In short, as not all words can be verbally defined, so not all knowledge can be explicated.

What sort of things can be said to be examples of tacit knowledge? Bodily and perceptual skills exemplify tacit knowledge. All of us walk, swim, shoot basketballs, and the like without being able to articulate fully this knowledge in words. In addition, we all are able to recognize another person's face in a crowd of thousands without being able to say how we do it. A more complex and much more important example of tacit knowledge would be the ability to grasp the concept of "meaning." Child and philosopher alike are unable to be fully explicit about the meaning of the term "meaning," but it is obvious that they each know what it means. In fact, one must know what "means" means before one can ask the question "What does 'means' mean?" And then the question is unnecessary. One way of accounting for this "logical primitiveness" of meaning is in terms of the concept of tacit knowledge.

One aspect of tacit knowlege that bears special mention is that which pertains to the role of the body. As was emphasized at the outset, it is necessary to view bodily activity as a form of cognitive judgment. Another way of putting this is to maintain that our bodies function as instruments for the attainment of knowledge which is often tacit in nature. This tacit knowlege is of necessity more closely related to bodily awareness and activity. Motor knowledge, for instance, can be obtained only by means of what Polanyi calls "indwelling." The only way to know some things is to indwell or participate in them. Now, since all knowledge is to some extent tacit, it becomes apparent that indwelling is an important aspect of every cognitive situation. There is always a sense in which the process of coming to know anything, be it an object or a person, is dependent upon empathetic indwelling.[4]

A summary of the concept of tacit knowledge thus far presented is now in order. Knowledge is to be viewed as a continuum between the tacit and explicit poles. All cognitive situations involve a blending of these two polar factors. Explicit knowledge is defined as a function of focal awareness and conceptual (or verbal) activity. As such it exhibits such characteristics as precise analysis, verbal articulation, descriptive identification, observational objectivity, and a clear distinction between the knower and the known (subject and object). Tacit knowledge, on the other hand, is defined as a function of subsidiary awareness and bodily activity. As such it exhibits such characteristics as intuitive discovery, bodily expression, holistic recognition, embodied subjectivity, and contextual distinction between the knower and the known.

The importance of the indwelling, as well as the general structure and pattern of tacit knowing, makes quite clear the degree to which and the sense in which the post-critical understanding of knowledge is dependent on the concept of participation. The standard dichotomy between "knowing how . . ." and "knowing that . . ." collapses, since the former, as embodied in tacit knowing, turns out to be the foundation for the latter.

SUBJECTIVITY, OBJECTIVITY, AND BEYOND

Generally speaking, the issue addressed by the foregoing distinction between explicit and tacit knowing is treated under the rubric of the dichotomy between objectivity and subjectivity. Whatever claims can be stated in clear and precise terms and/or inferences (whether inductive or deductive) can be rigorously tested for truth apart from any personal value judgments are said to provide "objective knowledge." Those claims, or "pseudo claims," which cannot meet these standards are said to be "merely subjective" value judgments. In other words, whatever notions, data, and claims can be focused explicitly qualify as knowledge, while those which cannot are relegated to the limbo of hunch, intuition, emotive, and noncognitive expressions. The concept of tacit knowledge is eliminated by definition at the outset.

What is not faced by the critical proponents of this objective-subjective dichotomy is the relativity inherent within it. For such an absolute distinction is possible only when very rigid definitions are set up and adhered to, but such rigidity can be established only by *arbitrary stipulation*. The various aspects and features of experience, like the different terms and utterances comprising language, do not come to us already regimented into ready-made objective and subjective compartments. Although there may be good reasons for dividing them up this way in specific circumstances for specific purposes, it must always be remembered that these divisions are relative to *our* stipulations, circumstances, and purposes.[5]

To get even more specific, any concept, no matter how carefully defined, can be given only a relative degree of precision. Mathematical quotients (such as π) as well as perceptual terms (such as "hot," "red," etc.) cannot be defined absolutely, but only in terms of so many decimal places or degrees on a spectroscope. In the same fashion, verification itself is dependent on previously stipulated definitions *and* can be carried on only within the confines of the context specified thereby. In fact, critical philosophers have had to admit that the notion of verification must be traded in for the more flexible notion of "confirmation," and that even this concept is applicable only in terms of degrees of probability. Thus it turns out that the much-trumpeted ideal of absolute objectivity is a Pickwickian notion, not because of human and/or technological limitations but because of the logical structure of definitions and verification procedures.

To put the above points positively, the realization and acknowledgment of the contextual character of the distinction between objective and subjective elements in the knowing process allow for a transcending of the schizophrenia which characterizes so much of Western culture. The antecedent conceptual and valuational framework provides the background and external context within which internal focus, definition, and confirmation can take place. Rather than being opposed, the so-called objective and subjective elements, the "factual" and the "valuational," are now seen as related functionally. In every knowing situation we attend to what is known explicitly (objectively) from what is known tacitly (subjectively).

It is in this way that the importance of the participatory dimension of the knowing process once again comes to the fore. The whole business of moving from our various commitments, purposes, and conceptual frameworks to a more articulated and controlled internal context highlights the extent to which our knowing is dependent on our involvement. *We,* after all, are the ones who have to *seek* knowledge, *we* have to believe that it is obtainable, *we* have to establish definitions and procedures for acquiring it, and *we* have to make judgments as to when it has been actualized. Moreover, our involvement at each of these levels is not something to be tolerated, but is rather the *sine qua non* of the very knowing process itself.[6]

Another way of looking at this fundamental relationship between the factual and the valuational dimensions of knowledge is to think of them as the dual, symbiotic foci of a single entity or dynamic. Even as the positive and negative poles of a magnetic field can only be defined and understood in relation to each other, so too with factual judgments and value judgments. The difference between these two situations is that there exists a vectorial relation running from the valuational toward the factual, because the former is logically though not experientially prior to the latter. Without a prior framework there can be no focus, without a place to come *from* there can be no place to go *to*. In our experience, to be sure, we move back and forth in cyclical fashion from the one to the other, and at this level the two are symbiotic and form a bipolar unity.

Frequently the very possibility of the logical priority of the valuational dimension of existence over the factual or "objective" dimension causes philosophers to despair of knowledge altogether. It is often assumed that if there is no ultimate, objective basis for knowledge, then it is impossible, since all else is "mere subjectivity" or at best a matter of "convention." The main thrust of a post-critical epistemology is to provide a way of avoiding this dilemma by developing a third and more fundamentally sound alternative. Rather than viewing knowledge as either objective or impossible, we are asked to view it as the result of a process of human activity in which we bring our commitments, capacities, and judgments to bear on our experience by interacting with the various dimensions and features of our multileveled reality.

What then provides the final justification for, the bedrock of, our knowledge? Hume and his contemporary followers sought such a final resting place in the combination of reason and sensory experience, but were unsuccessful. Kant and his followers sought it in the structure of the mind, but paid the price of eliminating from the cognitive domain many notions and issues that seem to be crucial to human existence. What is basic to understand is that there can be no ultimate justification of knowledge beyond or outside the human knowing process. Apart from the patterns and structure of participatory interaction there can be no knowledge at all. And, contrary to Kant's controlled skepticism, these patterns and this structure relate as much to questions about value, God, and human destiny as they do to questions about time, space, and causality. When our definition of meaningful questions excludes those which the vast majority of humanity, both past and present, find it necessary to deal with, then it is time to reconsider the definition.

The final justification of human knowledge lies not in objectivity, as with critical philosophy, nor in subjectivity, as with existentialism, but in our common and shared activity as knowing agents. Such activity is neither objective nor subjective, neither absolute nor merely conventional, for we neither transcend our epistemological situation, nor are we victimized by it. Rather, our knowing activity is simply and profoundly part and parcel of our way of "being-in-the-world," of our common "form of life." In response to critical philosophy's worry over the justification of induction as the final bedrock of human knowledge, Wittgenstein says:

> If anyone said that information about the past could not convince him that something would happen in the future, I should not understand him. One might ask him: What do you expect to be told, then? What sort of information do you call a ground for such a belief? What do you call "conviction"? In what kind of way do you expect to be convinced?—If these are not grounds, then what are grounds?—If you say these are not grounds, then you must surely be able to state what must be the case for us to have the right to say that there are grounds for our assumption.[7]

The Morality of Knowledge

Within the creed subscribed to by critical philosophers it is considered irresponsible, if not immoral, for one to commit oneself to anything of which one cannot be certain. Even after high probability has been substituted for certainty, the requirement of making commitment strictly proportionate to evidence remains in effect. The results of employing this notion of responsibility with respect to an overall epistemology are devastating in two directions at once. In one direction the criterion leads to making an idol of objectivity, since it is assumed that it alone can ensure that belief and commitment do not become overextended. But the necessary and positive function of personal involvement in the knowing process, as explored in the present chapter, renders obvious the naiveté and pernicious character of such idolatry. In the other direction the criterion of proportionate belief leads toward relativism and skepticism because it is assumed that since certainty, or even high probability, is either altogether impossible or is limited to areas of experience which are not essentially significant.

A careful consideration of the structure and dynamic of the knowing process reveals, however, that the standard for responsible belief employed in critical philosophy not only is impractical but is fundamentally out of harmony with those principles which constitute knowing. For a person to limit commitment in terms of certainties or high probabilities not only makes it impossible for the person to carry out many activities essential to the business of being human, but it is self-stultifying as well. For the very act of affirming *any* criterion for responsible belief at all, including the one proposed by critical philosophy, is an act which both makes a universal claim to being right and goes beyond that for which one can be said to have adequate "evidence." Moreover, each and every act of seeking knowledge implicitly involves an affirmation of the reality of knowledge, an affirmation that can neither be established nor debunked by rational and/or empirical procedures *because both such efforts presuppose it!*

Rather than seek to construct an objective criterion of knowledge and responsible belief, one external to the knower and the knowing process itself, and rather than despair because no such criterion can be constructed, we ought simply to affirm those commitments which render the search for truth possible and meaningful. This would mean that we *affirm* the reality of a structured and knowable world, and that we *accredit* our capacities and judgments for interacting with it. Moreover, the goals and standards that we must necessarily employ in such affirmations and accreditations also must be acknowledged as absolutes whose veridical character is not established by but underlies the knowing process.

Return to the bipolar symbiotic model for understanding the relationship between objectivity and subjectivity. It is the necessity of *personal* commitments to the reality of the world and knowledge which makes it impossible for objectivity to stand on its own. Likewise, it is the fact that these personal affirmations are made to reality and truth as *absolutes,* a phenomenon Polanyi calls "universal intent," which renders subjectivity inadequate. There is no knowledge apart from its affirmation by a particular knower in a particular time and place. Likewise, even the claim that knowledge is relative or impossible embodies the affirmation that *this* claim is true in an absolute sense. Thus both personal backing and universal intent are constitutive of knowledge; the former guards against objectivism, while the latter guards against subjectivism.

The fundamental contention of critical philosophy is that each and every aspect of the knowing process must be identified, analyzed, and evaluated *before* we are entitled to give assent to it. Our examination of the knowing process as grounded in tacit acts of integration has shown, however, that such critical analysis is neither possible, necessary, nor desirable. For such analysis itself embodies commitments to values which neither have been nor can be given prior scrutiny because they themselves are logically prior to such scrutiny. In a word, our acceptance of the values, standards, and judgments involved in the knowing process is and must be *acritical*, not critical. In this sense we find it necessary to "believe in order to understand." As Wittgenstein put it in *On Certainty*, "Knowledge is in the end based on acknowledgement."[8]

There are three main reasons why it is vitally important to replace a critical approach to epistemology with a post-critical approach. The first is that from a philosophical perspective, in the interest of constructing an adequate account of what it means to know, it is imperative not to leave out facets and dimensions that are crucial. Critical philosophy has been more concerned to define knowledge in terms of its preconceived ideas than in terms of actual experience. The second reason is that when an entire culture adopts and operates, however subliminally, on the basis of an epistemological posture which is self-defeating, the results are as far-reaching as they are disastrous. Many of the specialization gaps and moral dilemmas of our age are a direct result of our implicit commitment to the fact/value dichotomy. Thirdly, when one bases the search for knowledge, in whatever field, on a faulty model of what actually constitutes knowledge, then it would not be surprising if the results turned out to be misleading.

In all of this it is important that we keep in mind that the search for and legitimization of knowledge take place within a social context, or community. Individuals working within this context help, challenge, and confirm one another with the overall result of mutual personal accrediting and shared universal intent. Polanyi summarizes the dynamic of this participatory process as follows:

> While the logic of assent merely showed that assent is an a-critical act, commitment was introduced from the start as a framework in which assent can be responsible, as distinct from merely egocentric or random. The centre of tacit assent was elevated to the seat of responsible judgment. It was granted thereby the faculty of exercising discretion, subject to obligations accepted and fulfilled by itself with universal intent. A responsible decision is reached, then, in the knowledge that we have overruled by it conceivable alternatives,

for reasons that are not fully specifiable. Hence to accept the framework of commitment as the only situation in which sincere affirmations can be made, is to accredit in advance (if anything is ever to be affirmed) affirmations against which objections can be raised that cannot be refuted. It allows us to commit ourselves on evidence which, but for the weight of our own personal judgment, would admit of other conclusions. We may firmly believe what we might conceivably doubt; and may hold to be true what might conceivably be false.[9]

8

POST-CRITICAL
PHILOSOPHY

In Part One, I traced the main emphases of critical philosophy with respect to the crucial notions of experience, meaning, and knowledge, together with their implications for philosophy of religion. In Part Two, I presented fresh and more fruitful understandings of these crucial notions as the basis for a post-critical philosophy of religion. In Part Three, I shall develop post-critical explorations of these notions viewed from a religious perspective, with special emphasis on revelation, God talk, and confirmation. Before I move on to this task, however, it will prove useful to focus the post-critical stance more clearly by placing it in reference to the major philosophical postures on the contemporary scene. Such is the concern of the present chapter.

CRITICAL PHILOSOPHY APPRAISED

It is of utmost importance to distinguish a post-critical stance from a pre-critical one. The burden of this entire study has been to advocate, not a return to the philosophic perspective of classical or medieval times, but a fresh formulation of the central concepts that would both incorporate the insights of critical philosophy and transcend its counterproductive aspects. To the extent that pre-critical philosophy was based in a dualistic understanding of experienced reality (natural and supernatural), linguistic meaning (literal and allegorical), and knowledge (reason and faith) the revolution effected by critical philosophy has served as a most helpful corrective. The emphasis on this world, conceptual precision, and especially the cruciality of *inferential processes* have indeed made important contributions, both to philosophy in general and to philosophy of religion in particular.

The concern of Descartes, along with other rationalists, was to rescue knowledge from the confines of authority and tradition by stressing deductive inference as a self-critical process. This represents a commendable intention and a profound insight. Not only does deductive inference render the attainment of knowledge a public and replicable process but it carries with it a valuable stress on clarity and precision. These contributions were as necessary in theological and religious thought as they were in philosophy proper.

At the same time, the empiricist emphasis on experience as the source and test of all knowledge was also a much-needed ally in the task of overcoming the tyranny of authority and tradition. Here, too, the stress was on making knowledge more accessible and checkable by focusing on the role of inference, albeit inductive inference in this case. Moreover, empiricism and rationalism served as checks on one another in this liberation enterprise, each criticizing the other for being myopic in its understanding of understanding. Experience and reason were set against each other in their mutual attack on pre-critical thought.

Kant, of course, devised a way of integrating the insights of rationalism and empiricism, and in many ways his work stands as the high-water mark of critical philosophy. Not only did Kant employ both precise analysis and inferential reason in the structure as well as the content of his philosophy but he effectively eliminated speculation about knowledge and reality as extending beyond the human situation. However, his major contribution was his insight into the active character of the mind in the construction of knowledge and the constitution of experienced reality. This "Copernican revolution" stands as the cornerstone of both critical philosophy and post-critical philosophy. However, while he did stress the contribution of the mind in the construction of experienced reality, Kant did this in a "mentalistic" and "passive" manner (for the most part ignoring the role of the body), as I pointed out in Chapter 1.

The point, then, is not to seek a return to pre-critical thought, but to gauge the worth of critical insight, while being sensitive to its own inherent limitations, so as to be able to formulate an even more fruitful model of experience, meaning, and knowledge. The main concerns of critical philosophy remain well taken in their own right and in the historical context within which they arose. The difficulty lies in the fact that in its own way critical philosophy has become every bit as tyrannical as its predecessor had been. It has replaced a vague and dualistic posture with a narrow and reductionistic one. In a word, the critical posture represents a distortion of the concepts of experience, meaning, and knowing essentially as dysfunctional as that resulting from the pre-critical stance.

In its efforts to provide a complete explication of experience critical philosophy resorted to an atomistic model, which did away with traditional dualism but left us with a one-dimensional account of an obviously complex and variegated phenomenon. For all its talk of the finality of experience, empiricist philosophy is far more rationalistic in its stance than at first meets the eye. It strains experience through a preconceived sieve every bit as arbitrary and misleading as both pre-critical thought on the one hand and rationalism on the other. Far from fitting its theory of experience to life as lived, critical thought forces life to fit its theory. The result is distortion.

Similarly, the effort to ground linguistic meaning in experience led critical philosophers to draw the definition of meaningfulness so narrowly that it not only excluded much that was of interest and value but it excluded its own definition of meaningfulness as well. Here again the corrective action evolved into a reactionary posture which in the end nullified the gains. The cure turned out to be as bad as, if not worse than, the disease. The richness and open-textured character of linguistic meaning was lost in the drive for absolute precision. Once more, critical philosophy failed to fit its theory to actual practice and thereby distorted its own insights.

The same pattern obtained with respect to the critical approach to knowledge. The demand for complete explication and justification of all knowledge claims brought with it a skepticism or conventionalism which is completely out of harmony with the very possibility as well as the actuality of knowing. The insight that explanation and justification are necessary to the establishment of truth must be matched by the awareness that explanation and justification necessarily come to an end. This end is not, however, an arbitrary or conventional point of departure, but is rather the bedrock provided by the structure and character of the knowing process. The critical account of knowledge pretends that every reason can be explicated and justified on the basis of something other than or "beneath" itself. Surely this is self-defeating. As Wittgenstein put it in *On Certainty,* "The difficulty lies in being willing to begin at the beginning. And not try to go further back."[1]

EXISTENTIALISM REVISITED

Amid the monopoly acquired by critical philosophy on the concepts of reason, truth, and meaning it was not surprising that a movement would arise in protest. Thus existentialism. The attempt to reduce experience and truth to an analysis of data and evidence, to give an exhaustive and systematic account of life and meaning in terms of logical limits and objective verifiability outraged such thinkers as Nietzsche, Dostoevsky, and Kierkegaard—and rightly so. What these thinkers sought was a broader and deeper understanding of knowledge and truth, but since these notions had already been monopolized by critical thought (in both its empiricist and rationalist manifestations), the only course of action that seemed open to them was to declare themselves in favor of *"irrationalism."*[2] The point of this term is to stress the "absurd" character of human experience and the *subjective* quality of knowledge.

My own contention is that existentialist thinkers are motivated by the proper instincts but lack the conceptual tools necessary to come to grips with critical philosophy. This lack leads them to strike an irrationalist posture in order to protest against the epistemological "rip-off" they sensed taking place. The necessary conceptual tools have now been developed by such thinkers as Wittgenstein, Merleau-Ponty, and Polanyi, and thus the means are available for dismantling critical philosophy before it gets off the ground, without having to embrace irrationalism.

An examination of the standard interpretation of Kierkegaard not only will serve as an excellent case in point but will focus the special relevance of this issue for the philosophy of religion as well. I refer to the "standard" interpretation of Kierkegaard because I am of the opinion that his thought is generally misinterpreted, and that this fact itself illustrates the point I wish to make about the relationship between existentialism and post-critical philosophy. I shall conclude this section with a brief presentation of a different, and I believe more adequate, interpretation of Kierkegaard's work. This interpretation sees him as an ally of post-critical philosophy.

The standard view of Kierkegaard places him over against any and all attempts to explain experience in general and religious experience in particular in terms of objective reason. He is seen as protesting against objectivity as both an impossible and a misleading ideal because it is circular (i.e., it can only be justified by assuming it) and because it ignores the necessary role of commitment in both knowledge and life. The Kierkegaard of the *Philosophical Fragments* and the *Concluding Unscientific Postscript* argues against the possibility of any knowledge at all apart from the "subjective" involvement of the individual. Indeed, he contends that knowledge *per se* is impossible with respect to everything that matters—namely, value and meaning in life. Thus he follows Kant in making an absolute dichotomy between what can be known (the phenomenal world) and what cannot (the noumenal world), doing away in the latter with knowledge "in order to make room for faith."[3]

In effect Kierkegaard is interpreted as granting critical philosophy exclusive rights to the concepts of knowledge, reason, and fact, in order to make a case for the priority of commitment, faith, and valuation. In so doing, not only did he provide a profound analysis of the major dimensions of our ethical and emotional existence but he brought to bear some devastating criticisms of critical philosophy as well. While the major thrust of his critique was aimed at the rationalism of Hegel, a number of important blows were directed also at empiricism (especially at its exclusive reliance on sense-data and probability). The positive results of Kierkegaard's position are said to lie in the fields of ethics, aesthetics, psychology, and religion.

This standard interpretation of Kierkegaard is applied to the philosophy of religion in the following way. Since there is no possibility of obtaining objective knowledge in those areas of our lives, especially in the religious, which count the most, the only criterion of authenticity is that of subjective commitment. The degree to which a person is personally involved in his or her religion, the extent of "appropriation," is what constitutes truth (being "in the truth") with respect to religion. God cannot be *known* in the objective sense; he can be *believed in* only by means of a "leap of faith." Moreover, since belief in the paradoxical requires the greatest amount of faith, the religious claim that is the most paradoxical can be said to be the most "true." The Christian claim that "God was in Christ," that Jesus was both fully God and fully human, is the ultimate paradox, and thus the ultimate religious truth, and it is to be embraced by faith though not understood by reason.

Nonreligious existentialists, of course, part company from Kierkegaard when he moves from his initial analysis of the human situation to his application of it to religion. They argue that faith is a crutch which keeps people from assuming full responsibility for their own existence, and that truly authentic commitment involves no transcendent reference. Kierkegaard, as usually interpreted, would reply that such a horizontal understanding of life is defective because it pretends that humans are more than limited creatures. But this is an "in-house" debate and does not negate the unity among existentialist thinkers on the basic subjective character of existence and commitment.

My own contention is that while the irrationalist posture is both understandable and effective as a protest against critical philosophy, it remains as one-sided and limited in its own way as does the position to which it stands opposed. Not only is it unfortunate that we are forced to choose between those two alternatives which dominate the contemporary market but it is unnecessary as well. The construction of a post-critical philosophy provides yet a third alternative within which the insights of the opposing postures can be incorporated and the shortcomings set aside. The rationale for this post-critical approach is based on the essential impossibility of the dilemma resulting from the objective/subjective dichotomy offered by both critical and existentialist thinkers. In life it is impossible to choose between these two poles of our existence, and thus it is clear that the dominant positions do not exhaust the alternatives.

In conclusion I would also suggest that the standard interpretation of Kierkegaard is essentially wrongheaded, that he is better understood as a protest against the objective/subjective dichotomy than as an exponent of one side of it.[4] There are three main lines of support which can be offered for this interpretation. One pertains to the pseudonymous authorship of Kierkegaard's philosophical works, another to the content of these works themselves, and a third to Kierkegaard's own remarks about the relationship between his authorship and the notion of "indirect communication" (in *The Point of View for My Work as an Author*).

The standard interpretation completely ignores the obvious, and to Kierkegaard important, fact that all of his philosophical works (including *Fear and Trembling* and *Sickness Unto Death*) are attributed to fictitious characters who themselves do not claim to offer the final word and with whom Kierkegaard refuses to identify himself. Indeed, each of them claims and is said to represent a particular stage in or perspective on the road to truth. Moreover, the content of the works themselves is essentially self-contradictory in the sense that they constitute precisely what they not only claim *not* to offer but what they affirm is impossible—namely, an objective and systematic account of existence and religious faith. The irony of Kierkegaardian scholars quoting from pseudonymous authors as if they each spoke for Kierkegaard in order to set forth his "Existential System" (which he claims is impossible) would be comic if it were not so tragic.

The contradictory nature of the content of his philosophical works (including and most especially the profuse use of Hegelianisms such as "the teleological suspension of the ethical") is far too blatant to have been unintentional on Kierkegaard's part. Few philosophers are capable of conceiving of, let alone sustaining, such duplicity in their work, but Kierkegaard clearly was. For he was not primarily a philosopher, or a theologian, but was essentially a literary artist who both preached and practiced what he called "indirect communication." He maintained that spiritual truth cannot be communicated in a straightforward manner, because it is thereby reduced to an object and distorted. Thus it can only be treated indirectly in artistic media so as to preserve and encourage the responsibility of the individual receiving it.[5]

In my opinion Kierkegaard constructed his entire pseudonymous authorship as an ironic *tour de force* for the purpose of debunking *both* critical philosophy *and* irrationalism in one and the same move. The *content* of his philosophical works shows rationalism and empiricism to be erroneous, while the *form* shows their opposite to be equally absurd. With both major alternatives thereby critiqued, the reader, that "solitary individual," is confronted with the necessity of devising yet a third, more authentic posture. With specific regard to religion, I think Kierkegaard is saying, albeit indirectly, that faith is *neither* merely commitment based on objective reasons *nor* merely commitment devoid of reasons. Rather, faith is a way of *life* which includes both reason and commitment but which cannot be reduced to either of them.

This interpretation of Kierkegaard may or may not be correct. If it is not, it is difficult to maintain a high level of respect for him, since he failed to see the inconsistent and one-sided character of his own work. If, however, this view is at least near the truth, then Kierkegaard can be counted as an ally in the quest for a fresh, post-critical philosophy of religion.

LINGUISTIC ANALYSIS RESHAPED

The early work of Ludwig Wittgenstein, in his *Tractatus Logico-Philosophicus,* is a serviceable representative, if not the hallmark, of many of the chief emphases comprising critical philosophy. This gives special significance to the fact that his later work constitutes a radical critique of and departure from the critical approach to philosophy. The way of doing philosophy that has evolved out of the later Wittgenstein's thought, provocatively presented in his *Philosophical Investigations* and his *On*

Certainty, has come to be known as "linguistic analysis" or "ordinary language philosophy." Although many of its practitioners have failed to grasp the truly revolutionary thrust of Wittgenstein's mature work, tending to fall back upon pre-Wittgensteinian modes of analysis, there are excellent reasons for interpreting Wittgenstein himself as a progenitor of post-critical philosophy.

As has been indicated in earlier chapters, Wittgenstein's treatment of such notions as precision and rationality has a distinctly commonsense or pragmatic flavor, thereby undercutting the priority of critical analysis with respect to experience, meaning, and knowledge. His general procedure is to affirm the *primordial character* of the "ordinary" or everyday ways of speaking and thinking, since any sort of analytic refinement only becomes necessary and possible within the context or ground provided by them.[6] Thus such modes of speech and thought must be accepted and embodied *acritically* in order for any critical analysis and justification to take place. It is everyday speech and judgment which provide the criteria for constructing and evaluating more precise operations and locations, and not the other way around.

Parallel to the above concern is Wittgenstein's effort to stress the active and social quality of language and knowledge. His emphasis on language games as the matrix of meaning is aimed specifically at underlining the obvious but forgotten fact that language is *used* by persons to accomplish tasks, that speaking is something engaged in by active agents. Knowing, also, is a human activity which arises within the context of certain ways of speaking and acting, it is a way of *doing.* Wittgenstein's ultimate appeal is to what he calls "the human form of life," for at the bedrock level what human beings incorporate into their way of life is what comes to be called true and meaningful.[7] Such criteria "show themselves" in the dynamics or weave of our corporate existence, even though they may not be articulatable by means of critical analysis.[8]

The understanding of philosophy which is concomitant with this *a*critical approach to such central notions as meaning and knowledge reaches far beyond the typical stereotype of Wittgenstein's thought as "mere epistemological handwashing" without retreating to the traditional, pre-critical understanding of philosophy as a solution-producing "super-science." To my mind the best term with which to characterize it was suggested by J. L. Austin—namely, *"linguistic phenomenology."*[9] For by means of his explorations of the "depth grammar" of linguistic usage

Wittgenstein seeks to lay bare the structure of the relationship among thought, persons, and the world. Although it is clear that he has not provided anything like a complete "surfacing" of this structure, it is equally as clear that he has made a revolutionary and lasting contribution to the development of a post-critical philosophy.

It is significant in this regard to reflect on the character of the personal experiences and background out of which his earlier, critical philosophy and his later, post-critical thought came. His early training was in engineering, including both the scientific and the mathematical aspects. The work of Russell and G. Frege served, along with that of Schopenhauer, as the catalyst for the construction of his logical analysis and atomism. During his "retirement" from philosophy he spent fifteen years engrossed in such *common and practical activities* as gardening, housebuilding, and schoolteaching. These experiences, especially the latter, provided a vantage point for seeing the logical priority of ordinary speech and activity over abstract, critical analysis. Life and its daily tasks provide the context for critical thought, and thus its criteria and justification, and not the other way around.

Perhaps the most clear-cut indication of the post-critical quality of Wittgenstein's later work is the mode within which he conducts and presents his explorations. Rather than continue in the argumentative and/or analytic style of both traditional and critical philosophy, Wittgenstein shifts in his later work to what is best termed the *metaphoric mode*.[10] Hardly any attention whatsoever has been given to the fact that the means of persuasion employed in *Philosophical Investigations* and *On Certainty* is not that of argumentation but that of exploration and invitation. Wittgenstein offers example after example and encourages the reader to reflect on and engage these concrete cases. His own reasoning process progresses from one striking and provocative metaphor to the next. Critical philosophers and traditional philosophers alike have expressed exasperation over this manner of doing philosophy; but not only does it yield important results, it can be shown to underlie all other approaches as well, including the critical approach.[11]

It must be acknowledged that the foregoing interpretation of Wittgenstein is a bit out of step with the standard view as well as with the actual work of many of his so-called "followers." To my way of thinking, most self-styled "post-Wittgensteinians" actually continue to philosophize within the limitations of a pre-Wittgensteinian (critical) perspective. Many ordinary language philosophers, as is traditional with British thinkers, reflect the clarity of Wittgenstein's thought without reflecting any of its profundity. A quick perusal of the current English-speaking journals of philosophy will substantiate this judgment. While they contain many genuine post-critical insights, even the works of such brilliant thinkers as Gilbert Ryle, J. L. Austin, Peter Strawson, and Max Black, all exhibit the tendency to assume that a final and complete analysis of a given concept or problem can and must be arrived at. The thinker who extends the Wittgensteinian approach most faithfully and revealingly is John Wisdom. His *Paradox and Discovery* is a classic example of post-critical philosophy. In it he affirms the logical priority of wholeness to analysis in experience, meaning, and knowledge, suggesting that metaphorical understanding is the mode most appropriate to surfacing the structure of reality.

PHENOMENOLOGY REVISED

The movement known as phenomenology takes as its starting point the work of Edmund Husserl.[12] Husserl sought to construct a philosophical approach that would set aside or "bracket" the traditional debates between realists and skeptics because such debates led philosophers into blind alleys. Rather than begin by affirming or denying the truth of our judgments about the existence and nature of the world, the self, and others, Husserl proposed to begin by examining the data of perception and experience as *given* or as *lived,* quite apart from theoretic interpretations. He proposed a "science" of the "raw" *phenomena* of experience. In his later work there is evidence that Husserl came to see the naive, even "positivistic," tone of his original program, acknowledging that a "neutral" vantage point is both impossible and unnecessary.[13] It has remained, however, for more recent phenomenologists to work out the implications of this more sophisticated approach.

Husserl's most important contribution pertains to the notion of *intentionality,* by which he called attention to two deeply important qualities of human experience and consciousness. The first is simply that our awareness of our world is always a function of our *interaction* with or participation in it. The world is neither received nor understood through passive observation, but only through engagement. Secondly, our awareness of the world has a vectorial or directional ($\longrightarrow$) quality to it, that is, our consciousness is always *consciousness of* something. This means that we cannot come to understand our experience or our knowledge of it in the abstract, but only *as* we engage some meaningful aspect of and within our lives *as experienced*. The *intentional* character of our experienced reality entails that the only aspects of reality we can experience and know are those to which we can relate as meaningful wholes. The value of these insights for a post-critical philosophy, as outlined in the previous chapter, can hardly be overestimated.

Unfortunately, as is the case with linguistic philosophy, those who have taken up the cause instituted by the "father" of the phenomenological movement have frequently allowed themselves to "backslide" into patterns of approach and thought which both predate and obviate post-critical insights. Phenomenologists often become quite *introspective* and *rationalistic* in their method, going on and on with systematic classifications of the "data" of (presumably) their own experience without pausing to provide any common, intersubjective means by which others can confirm or disconfirm their assertions.[14] As linguistic philosophers exhibit both the advantages (clarity, rigor, etc.) and the disadvantages (superficiality, skepticism, etc.) of doing philosophy in the "English-speaking mode," so phenomenologists reflect the merits (profundity, comprehensiveness, etc.) and the liabilities (abstractness, dogmatism, etc.) of doing philosophy in the "Continental mode."

To my way of thinking, the phenomenologist who provides the greatest amount of insight for the least amount of mystification is Maurice Merleau-Ponty. Two major contributions stemming from his work warrant pinpointing. The first pertains to the characterization of the phenomeno-logical method. Avoiding the pitfalls of "objectivism," even that implied by Husserl's early writings, and those of "subjectivism," exhibited by existentialism, Merleau-Ponty both preaches and practices a truly phenomenological understanding of experienced reality. Claiming neither to examine the structures of the world and our knowledge of it *directly,* nor to be unable to understand them at all, he affirms a posture which seeks to understand understanding *as* it is engaged with the world and to understand the world *as* engaged. Granting that we cannot and need not disengage ourselves, he maintains that we can "loosen the threads"[15] or *shift the gears* of our intentionality and gain thereby an understanding of both our own nature and that of the world.

The second major contribution resulting from Merleau-Ponty's work is the emphasis on the cruciality of *the body* to our experience and knowledge of the world. Whereas almost all traditional and critical philosophers, and the vast majority of existentialists as well, have systematically ignored or denigrated the body's role in human existence, Merleau-Ponty argues a thoroughly documented and convincing case for its pivotal importance. In his book *Phenomenology of Perception*[16] he establishes and clarifies the place of the body in perception, thought, language, sexuality, and knowledge of the self, the world, and others. The significance of this somatic understanding of experience, meaning, and knowledge for the post-critical postures sketched out in Part Two of this present work should be obvious.

In addition, the connections should be clear between the importance of the body in Merleau-Ponty's philosophy and (1) the role of *action* in existentialist, especially Kierkegaardian thought, (2) the idea of language as grounded in human *social activity* in Wittgenstein's later work, and (3) the centrality of *somatic indwelling* to Polanyi's concept of tacit knowing. Moreover, there are strong and valuable connections among all these thinkers with respect to the axial character of intention and meaning in all human experience. Finally, there is a common concern among them to insist upon the necessity of dimensions of reality and knowledge which can and need only to be *shown* rather than *said*. On the basis of these points of confluence I have sought to alter the axis of philosophical understanding with respect to the concepts of experience, meaning, and knowledge. The next task is to explore the ramifications of this axial shift for the philosophy of religion.

Part Three

POST-CRITICAL PHILOSOPHY
OF RELIGION

9

RELIGIOUS EXPERIENCE

Having sought to relocate our philosophical axis—from critical to post-critical thought—we now will explore the ramifications of such a shift for the philosophy of religion. The format of the next three chapters will be to begin this exploration with respect to the three central concepts of modern philosophy—experienced reality, linguistic meaning, and human knowledge—as they bear on religion. In each of the chapters the emphasis should be on the term "beginning exploration," since many of the ramifications remain undiscovered. The main task of this study has been to locate and alter the axis of modern thought. Searching out all the implications lies beyond the scope of this book.

The present chapter will treat the concept of religious experience and will revolve around the suggestions and notions introduced in Chapter 5. The central concern is to construct an interpretation of religious experience that (1) transcends the pitfalls of traditional dualism and reductionism, (2) maintains a continuity between general human experience and our experience of the divine, and (3) does justice to the tone and tenor of religious experience as known and affirmed by religious persons themselves. The focus will be on the Judeo-Christian understanding of religion.

As Dimensional

When experienced reality is thought of as dualistic (natural and supernatural realms), as with pre-critical thought, or as atomistic (sense-data and facts), as with critical philosophy, the concept of religious experience is treated accordingly. In the first instance it is generally thought of as an *intrusion* upon natural or commonplace experience, as a suspension of the regular structure and character of everyday life. Thus a great emphasis is placed on the "miraculous" and upon visitations from and visions of the supernatural or divine realm. From the point of view of Judeo-Christian theism, this way of looking at religious experience is problematic, though traditional, for two main reasons. One, it hinges on a strong contrast between the natural world and historical revelation, both of 'which come from the same God. Surely a more harmonious view of God's creative and revelatory activity must be found. Secondly, such a view fails to come to grips with the radical significance of the notion of *incarnation*. For at the heart of this notion lies the insight that the divine enters into the natural in an essentially nonobtrusive fashion. More on this in a bit.

According to the second interpretation mentioned above, the traditional dualistic, or two-story, world view is set aside and all experience is accounted for on the basis of a *horizontal model*. Thus, any claim to an experience of a "higher order," be it ethical, aesthetic, or religious, is reduced to an account of the particulars of sensory observation and empirical behavior. The realmistic perspective is exchanged for a flat perspective. As has been pointed out, the difficulties with this modern, atomistic packaging of experience are that not only does it fail to do justice to the complexity and richness of human existence but it even fails to provide a means of explaining and justifying its own point of view. If experience and reality are really *flat*, then there is no vantage point from which to see, let alone explain, that they *are* flat. This is the dilemma which faces all contemporary attempts to interpret religious experience humanistically, whether pro or con. Once the sense and possibility of transcendence has been eliminated, both the richness and the very viability of a meaningful and/or true understanding of existence are obviated.

In this way any attempt to provide a helpful treatment of religious experience is confronted with a dilemma. One should either do so in traditional, dualistic terms and find oneself stressing the divine as an intrusion on the natural, or one should construe religion humanistically and end up asking oneself where the richness went. It is my contention that the way of viewing experience proposed in Chapter 5 provides a way out of this dilemma by means of the idea of reality as mediated dimensions.

When experience is understood as essentially a relational, embodied, synaesthetic, and symbiotic reality, many of the difficulties that dog the two standard postures outlined above disappear. For in both cases the emphasis has been on understanding human experience in terms of a model that is static, mentalistic, isolated, and passive. The relational, embodied, synaesthetic, and symbiotic character of experience, as discussed in Chapter 5, can helpfully be brought together in the model of reality as mediated dimensions, which was also briefly introduced in that chapter.

The central idea here is that rather than think of experienced reality as divided up into stratified realms, or as strictly horizontal, it is most fruitful to think of it as comprised of a number of *simultaneously interpenetrating dimensions*.[1] The main point of such a proposal is to see that we live in all the major aspects of our existence at once and that each affects the other. Secondly, these dimensions of experience can be thought of as arranged according to a *hierarchy of richness* and *comprehensiveness*, beginning with the physical and moving on up through the social, the moral, the aesthetic, to the religious. Thirdly, these dimensions are experienced as *mediated* in and through one another, the richer and more comprehensive by means of the less so. This notion of mediation is crucial and warrants fuller treatment, especially as it pertains to religious experience.

Richer and more comprehensive aspects of experience are said to be mediated through the less so in the sense that we cannot become aware of them apart from the latter, but once we are aware of them it is clear that they cannot be explained fully in terms of the latter either. Our experience of the "higher" dimensions (*not* realms) of reality comes only *in and through* our interaction with the less complex and comprehensive dimensions, but it is not exhausted by such interaction. This mediational structure is common to every aspect of our experience, from the everyday business of comprehending meaning as expressed in the particulars of vocabulary, grammar, intonation, gesture, and situation, to such highly abstract activities as scientific theorizing and aesthetic criticism.

As the illustration at the close of Chapter 5 suggests, our moral awareness is helpfully understood as mediated in and through our physical awareness in the sense that while it does not arise apart from the latter, it does not constitute merely an addition to it either; it is more without being less. In the same way, aesthetic awareness comes by means of physical awareness without being reducible to it. Religious experience too, then, can be helpfully thought of as arising out of and yet transcending the physical, social, moral, and aesthetic dimensions of reality. The divine interpenetrates the other dimensions at all points, is mediated in and through them so as to be both transcendent and immanent.

This understanding of religious experience stresses, then, the continuity between human awareness in general and religious awareness in particular.

Both with respect to what is traditionally known as "general revelation" (God's self-disclosure in creation, available to all humans) and "special revelation" (God's self-disclosure within specific historical and sociopolitical circumstances), the notion of religious experience as structured dimensionally and mediationally carries with it the understanding that religious awareness is of a piece with other forms of human awareness without being reducible to them. Thus it escapes the dilemma posed by the more standard postures of dualism and atomism.

While the concept of general revelation is usually understood as stressing the continuity between our experience and our knowledge of the divine (often taken up under the rubric of "natural theology" or philosophical theology), this is not the case with special revelation. Here, traditionally, the stress has been on discontinuity. As I see it, however, this move systematically leads to conceptual dead ends concerning acceptable criteria for the recognition of special revelation. The incarnational or mediational emphasis I am urging on the present pages seeks to locate such criteria *within* the general experience of all humanity, especially in the social and historical dimensions. This still allows for a distinction between general and special revelation, since the former is traditionally worked out in relation to theological and moral considerations.

It should be pointed out in passing that since the perspective of this chapter focuses on the religious dimension *as experienced*, the stress is on the human side of divine-human interaction. No attempt is here made to negate the notions of God's initiative and continued activity in human lives. The concept of divine grace is essentially a theological one and not the proper concern of philosophy of religion. Suffice it to say that an interactionist understanding of religious experience not only leaves room for the notion of divine activity but indeed encourages and even may be said to entail it.

As Relational

The pivotal point of a dimensional understanding of religious experience is that of *interaction*. We become aware of and participate in the religious dimension of reality only when and as we engage it in searching, responding, deciding, and growing. Just as the moral and aesthetic dimensions of reality are not disclosed to us, go unnoticed by us, unless we are drawn to them through involvement and concern, through wondering, probing, and choosing, so too the religious dimension can only be encountered through interaction.[2]

Seeing the crux of religious experience in this way immediately draws attention to the contrast between a post-critical understanding and the two dominant traditional postures. On the one hand, religious experience conceived of as relational is entirely distinct from that posture which construes belief as mental *assent* to or affirmation of certain theological *propositions,* whether inferred, deduced, or revealed. On the other hand, the usual antidote to the above, some form of mysticism in which the believer is directly *confronted* with the divine, is also denied by an emphasis on relational interaction. For the latter focuses on a give-and-take dynamic which sees the divine as active, as taking initiative, and is to be interacted with in every dimension and situation of existence. The religious dimension transcends the other, less rich and comprehensive dimensions in the sense that it cannot be fully explained in terms of them, but it is immanent in each of them in the sense that it is mediated by each.

A relational, interactive view of religious experience also stands in direct contrast to the more popular and contemporary posture—namely, existentialism. For the latter stresses *commitment,* as an act of the *will,* as the pivot point of religious belief. This perspective is essentially unilateral in that it sees faith as originating in a vacuum, or at least from the human side. Thus it is to be distinguished from a relational understanding which sees religious faith and experience as a *mutual,* symbiotic involvement of disclosure and commitment. The divine comes to us in and through the other dimensions of our lives; through places, things, events, persons, and ideas, disclosing itself and calling for honest response.

The view of religious experience being proposed here is one wherein God is known, not by reason and inference as such, nor by feeling and/or commitment in and of themselves. Rather, God is known through *responding* to that which transcends yet is present in the experiential dimensions comprising human existence in general—namely, nature, persons, emotions, and ideas. Each dimension and context of our experience contains within itself, indeed is bounded by, an element of *mystery* which when responded to may be said to carry with it the potential for divine disclosure. This element of mystery is of course to be distinguished from as yet unsolved problems and/or lack of information in a given field.[3] It is, rather, to be thought of as that which *in principle* remains unexplainable within any dimension of experience, thus giving rise to an awareness of our own limitations and to the possibility of a transcendent dimension.

No general account can be given of the way in which this transcendent possibility becomes an experiential actuality, for then its transcendent and mysterious character would be obviated; which in principle is impossible, since no account can ever be exhaustive in the sense of explaining its own parameters and foundations. All that can be done is to stress the facts that (1) throughout history and among all cultures, including our own appearances to the contrary notwithstanding, human beings have found it helpful—necessary?—to make room in their life and thought (indeed, at the *center* of their life and thought) for the interpenetration of the natural dimensions of existence by a religious or transcendent dimension; and (2) it is fruitful to view the nature of this religious awareness as based in relational interaction between humans and the divine.

Not the least of the advantages of viewing religious experience as mediated dimensionally and through relationship is that it provides a structure for maintaining both human *freedom* and *responsibility*. That is to say, if religious awareness were direct rather than indirect, it would virtually eliminate the need for responsive commitment, in the same way as the (at least relatively) unmediated character of physical experience leaves little room for commitment or doubt (except among those inflicted with the disease known as critical philosophy). The other side of the coin is that relational mediation not only guarantees the *volitional space* within which a person is free to respond positively or negatively to mediated disclosures of the divine, but it also provides an *arena of engagement* which invites and encourages a person to interact with and participate in the religious dimension of existence. It is this possibility which is obviated by the existentialist insistence on "the leap of faith," for this places commitment in an experiential vacuum and fails to do justice to the activity (even though mediated) of the divine in the human situation.

Although no general or detailed account can be given of the particulars constituting the sort of response dynamic involved in a participatory, relational interaction with the divine dimension as mediated, perhaps an example will be of help. In the Western critical tradition we have come to assume that we must *know before we act,* but this is surely self-defeating as a policy and erroneous as a description. Action of some sort, involvement, precedes thought—and it must, logically speaking, since thought must begin somewhere. This does not make our primordial activity irrational; rather, it makes it the standard to which reason itself appeals and the very basis of human experience itself. Pascal knew this. Toward the close of his famous passage on "the wager" he offers a brief hint to those who would like to know how to move from unbelief to belief. He says: "Learn of those who have been bound like you and who now stake all their possessions. . . . Follow the way by which they began; by acting as if they believed, taking the holy water, having masses said, etc."[4]

Within whatever context we find ourselves, within whatever dimension of experience we are stimulated to engage those aspects which are both mysterious and fundamental, we are invited to interact with serious and honest involvement. It is at such interactive junctures that many have claimed—and *do* claim—that the divine dimension is disclosed. If such things as holy water and Masses seem relevant as modes of interaction, well and good. If other modes, such as prayer, change of life-style, and value commitments, seem more appropriate, fine. The point is, both seeking and finding are relational activities, for it is only through interaction that the religious dimension is experienced.

As Social and Historical

Throughout the foregoing discussion of the mediated and relational character of a post-critical understanding of religious experience there has been an unspecified but nonetheless crucial consideration which now needs to be brought into the foreground. So far the focus has been on the religious dimension as that which is mediated and now some attention must be given to the human dimension which serves as the primary mediator. Although the physical dimension of our experience is "square one" with respect to all other levels of mediation, and although the power and intelligence of the divine can rightfully be said to be revealed in nature, it remains true that the primary arena within which we encounter the divine is the human dimension. Without in any way pretending to be exhaustive, it is at least useful to think of the human dimension according to a twofold division—namely, the social and the historical.

Although we are accustomed in the West to think of the human dimension primarily in personal and individual categories, recent work in anthropology and social psychology has made it plain not only that most other cultures do not conceive of themselves in this way but that even in the highly individualized West the self is essentially a social phenomenon.[5] Incidentally, or perhaps not so incidentally for the overall theme of Part

One of this present book, there is a vital connection between the individualization and individualism of our heritage on the one hand and the atomism of modern, critical thought on the other hand. Both Cartesian dualism, to say nothing of Platonic dualism, and Lockean and/or Skinnerian reductionism begin by assuming that individualized selfs comprise the basic building blocks of the human situation.

To follow a post-critical mode of thought in a consideration of the way in which the religious dimension mediates itself in and through the human dimension means to adopt a "social interactionist" view of the latter instead of an atomistic view. Such a shift involves acknowledging at the outset that the self is better understood as a kind of fabric or magnetic field than as an indissoluble metaphysical unit or substance. At a primordial level we *are* our relationships; and our awareness of and participation in the various dimensions of human existence is to a large degree a function of our interaction with one another in community.[6] Thus even our knowledge of ourselves, to say nothing of our knowledge of physical and social reality, is mediated in and through our interaction with others.

When one comes at religious experience from this perspective the traditional approaches, whether in terms of strictly rational concepts and arguments or in terms of individualized mysticism or volitionalism, are revealed as entirely out of place. Religious awareness is mediated in and through our interaction within and among the social or community dimension of our existence. Beginning with our general awareness of the notion of a divine being as extant in our culture, on through the specifics of a particular religious tradition in which we participate, or choose *not* to participate, and even down to our most personal religious experiences and decisions—in all of these aspects of the divine dimension of our existence it is the social character of our way of "being-in-the-world" which mediates the religious to us. Not only is our religious cultural heritage a social phenomenon, but even our most personal religious decisions take place in an interpersonal and intersubjective matrix which establishes our expectations and alternatives.[7]

It is, then, crucial to see that religious experience as conceived post-critically is mediated socially. This means not only that religion is a social event and has a history but that whatever our experience of the divine consists in we are aware of it and respond to it within a community context. Religious commitment does not arise within, nor can it be given expression within, a personalized vacuum. This is not to deny that there is a personal pole within the social field of mediated experience, but it is crucial to maintain that the personal and social poles exist, are defined, and are experienced in relation to and in interaction with each other; and, moreover, that God is known in and through this fabric or field and not apart from it. The society, the cultural heritage, the institutionalized church, the denominational subcultures, even the cults and especially the family, are mediators of our awareness of the religious. God comes to us *through* them and we respond to God *within* them.

The second aspect of the human dimension of experience through which religious awareness is mediated is the historical. Not only do we exist within a multifaceted social network but this network has a past and a future. Therefore the events, places, and peoples of the past and the future are also mediators of the divine. Both the concrete happenings and the mythological frameworks of our own traditions, as well as those of other traditions, are inextricably bound up with the mediation of the religious dimension of reality. Likewise the goals, hopes, and fears which we project on the future not only reflect our present anticipations but they serve as mediators of our awareness in the present as well. For we interact with the various aspects of the present in the light of our future projections. The divine dimension is thus mediated in and through the historical.

The primary reason for the importance of the historical facet of the human dimension of experience as a mediator of religious awareness lies with the *embodied character of our existence* (as discussed in Chapter 5). Because we are in the world as bodies, the particulars of time, place, and event become vital to the formation of our experience and to our understanding. Although there is a sense in which we can be said to transcend the limitations of embodiment through imagination and invention, it remains true that such acts of transcendence are themselves rooted in and mediated through historical embodiment.

It is the awareness of the crucial role played by the historical dimension of human existence which uniquely characterizes the Judeo-Christian religious perspective. The notion that God is an active agent who enters into relationship with humans in and through the particulars of time, place, event, and persons is central to this perspective. The exodus and the incarnation function as the pivotal points around which the religious insights and experiences of this tradition revolve. In addition, the activity of God in the historical dimension is paradigmatically in and through the activity of persons, groups, and nations. Even for the contemporary Jew or

Christian the experience of God is largely mediated by the events that comprise their personal, social, and national existence. Perhaps the best model by means of which to grasp the cruciality and character of this general notion is that of revelation through the incarnation.

THROUGH A GLASS, DARKLY

The claim that "in Christ God was reconciling the world to himself" is central to the Christian faith and must then also be crucial to the notion of religious experience as understood within a Christian framework. In one way or another the religious experience of the Christian revolves around the activity of God, in both the world at large and the individual's life, as it is mediated in and through the person of Christ. Thus it behooves us to consider the nature of the incarnation as it bears on our understanding of the mediated structure of religious awareness.

To begin with, it is important for us to appreciate the highly *contextual* quality of the incarnation as presented in the New Testament. God is said to have come into our world, not as a mere apparition or disguised deity, but as an actual personage in a particular time, place, and sociopolitical situation. Nor is the incarnation a kind of divine superman pretending to be a mild-mannered Clark Kent. God is said to have become a real person, a fully human being and more. Not only does this understanding of the incarnation stand in marked contrast to the ways in which other religions speak of the visitations of their gods but it also stands opposed to the notion of revelation in the form of an abstract principle or truth, a kind of divine plan or message in propositional form. God's involvement in our world did not take the form of cosmic skywriting or international fireworks. Rather, it came in the concrete personal, social, and historical dimension of human existence.

Perhaps the most important feature of this contextuality aspect of the Christian concept of incarnation is that of *divine interaction* with humanity. God is portrayed as taking action on behalf of humankind, as entering into a reconciling relationship, as *loving* in such a way as to *give* fully of himself. The emphasis here is on God as *agent* and upon the possibility of humans responding to this divine activity in an affirmative and thorough fashion. Once again the post-critical theme of experience as relational can be seen to dovetail with an important consideration in the Christian understanding of God. In theology dominated by critical philosophy the interactionary themes of Christian thought were either translated into conceptual abstractions (omnipotence, omniscience, immutable, necessary, and the like), as with both the liberalism of the Enlightenment and the fundamentalism of the twentieth century, or they have been demythologized away ("mere Jewish eschatology") by existentialist theologians such as Bultmann.

A second important incarnational theme is that of *embodiment*. It is crucial not to overlook the implications of the Christian claim that God came into our form of life, our way of being-in-the-world, as an embodied person: "The Word became flesh." This makes it quite clear that in Christian thought and life there can be no simplistic identification between bodily existence and evil. This is a point theologians (e.g., Augustine) and preachers have frequently forgotten. Moreover, the embodied character of God's incarnational activity is necessarily connected with the Christian notion of bodily resurrection. This concern with the importance of embodiment not only suggests a positive appreciation of physical existence but it underlines the concrete quality of God's interaction with humanity. Revelation does not have to do with abstract truths, but with real persons in real life situations.

Furthermore, the notion of embodiment carries with it a sense of *vulnerability* and risk. Whenever one enters into relationship with others, a kind of self-limitation takes place; one is not in full control of the other person and thus runs the risk of misunderstanding or rejection. Moreover, real relationship involves a reciprocal dialogue in which both parties give and receive. The New Testament makes it plain that God's activity in Jesus Christ involved this sort of vulnerability and reciprocity. "He came to his own home, and his own people received him not." Jesus' life and death, as a suffering servant on behalf of others, embodied the characteristics that are essential to a relational, interactionary focus for a post-critical understanding of religious experience.

Finally, it is clear that the Christian concept of incarnation corresponds extraordinarily well with the post-critical notion of mediation.[8] God comes into our world indirectly, not directly (as with mysticism) or inferentially (as with critical thought). The very term "incarnation" carries with it the connotation of communication *in and through*, rather than direct manifestation, as well as the idea of embodiment rather than intellectual process. The special significance of the statement "The *Word* became flesh" lies in the fact, as we have repeatedly seen, that meaning is communicated in language by means of mediation. Meaning does not occur apart from words, but it is always more than words as well. In the same way, the religious dimension is mediated to us in and through the more concrete dimensions of our existence. Thus religious experience within the Christian framework is understood as mediational partly because the incarnation is itself paradigmatically mediational. As a result of God's activity in Jesus Christ we now are said to "see through a glass, darkly."

Both aspects of this last quotation from Paul are extremely important. In Christian experience we do see and interact with the divine dimension. The revelation in Christ is sufficient for those who seek. At the same time, we must remember that we only know God indirectly, as "in a mirror dimly." We can never claim to know God fully, nor to think or speak from the divine perspective. Our experience of God is mediated and relational, since it arises within the concrete context provided by the other dimensions of our existence. And the incarnation serves as a catalyst or axial point around which this mediation and interaction revolve.

This overall point can be seen in the manner with which Jesus is portrayed as dealing with those around him in the Gospels.[9] Consider how frequently he "answered" a question with another question, how almost exclusively he spoke in metaphor and especially parables. Further, it should not be forgotten that Jesus systematically avoided the various interpretations and titles which others were eager to place on him, and that the accounts of his post-resurrection appearances do not depict him as returning to those in power in order to vindicate himself. Jesus' way of being-in-the-world was itself oblique, as befits a mediational disclosure. He sought to draw others into reflection and decision about the basis and quality of their existence, and to create "space" within which they could be both free and responsible for such reflection and decision. His was a "soft sell" rather than a "hard sell."

10

RELIGIOUS LANGUAGE

Against the background of the foregoing discussion of religious experience as mediated and relational, the question arises, What sort of speech, what mode of linguistic expression, is most appropriate to this pattern of experience? To put the matter somewhat differently, given the axial shift from critical philosophy's interpretation of language as representation to a post-critical understanding of meaning as a function of use in context, what are the ramifications of this shift for the meaning of religious language? My overall concern is to show that a post-critical posture lifts the question of the meaning of "God talk" out of the cul-de-sac created for it by the rubrics supplied by contemporary critical philosophy.

Setting the Stage

To begin with, a number of general points need to be made as reminders of important considerations already treated. The first such point is that to a large degree religious reality and experience are *linguistically constituted,* even as life in general is linguistically constituted. We are initiated into the various dimensions and aspects of the world in which we live by becoming participants in what Wittgenstein called the "language games" appropriate to them. People speak to each other and to us, even when we are infants, in relation to physical objects, time, space, persons, values, relationships, ideas, etc., and as we are drawn into these conversations, these phenomena become real for us. This is *not* to say that none of these things would be real, or experienced, by organisms if there were no language, but it *is* to say that as a matter of fact none of them *do* become real for us apart from our becoming members of a speaking community. All human societies employ language as a chief means of dealing with, and introducing their offspring to, the world.[1]

Even those who are born deaf and dumb come to participate in the human world, the world as we know it, by being brought into language. Helen Keller referred to her prelingual self as "phantom," and she said that prior to coming to know language she did no "intentional" acts, but only responded to immediate stimuli. Psychologically induced aphasia and autism also bear witness to the cruciality of language in the constitution of human reality. Thus religious language, too, must be seen as a mediator of religious experience and reality. Only through exposure to and participation in talk *of* and *to* God, do we come to an encounter with the divine. This does not mean that everyone who is so exposed will become religious, but it does mean that no one participates in the religious dimension apart from linguistic activity, *and* that even those who neglect or reject religious experience do so in relation to its linguistic mode and in that sense *within* it.

A second important and related reminder pertains to the fact that language is a *social activity*. More specifically, speaking is something that people do in order to accomplish certain tasks within the warp and weft of human life. Thus language is a functional phenomenon whose meaning can only be grasped through its use within concrete and community-oriented contexts. It is a common fallacy, among both critical thinkers and common folk, that the primary, perhaps exclusive nature of speech is to describe (picture or represent!) facts or impart information. While this is an important function of language, it is hardly the exclusive or even primary one. For descriptions and information are not ends in themselves; they occur and are given within broader contexts as part of specific language games participated in by purposeful people for various ends.

The significance of this point for religious discourse is far-reaching and fundamental. Most of the difficulties that have arisen within the God talk debate have centered around the assumption that the sole and/or primary purpose of religious speech is to describe God. Not only are there other important uses of religious language, such as persuasion, confession, exaltation, exhortation, ritualization, and the like, but these uses generally outrank or provide the context for descriptions of God. Moreover, even when the primary purpose does seem to be a characterization of divine reality, as in the case of theology proper, the simplistic, flat understanding of description which underlies the critical approach to such utterances systematically obscures the entire issue.[2] The complexities of speech about moral and aesthetic value, subatomic physics, and conceptual reality ought to provide ample warning of, and even some clue to, the intricacies of talk about religious reality.

A third and final reminder. The meaningfulness of language is not dependent on precise definition and articulation, but rather it is based in *significant precision*. Absolute precision is not possible, since all definitions (including ostensive definitions) are ultimately based in previously undefined utterances and/or gestures. Nor is absolute precision necessary, since we do not learn to speak in the first place, nor are we able to participate in everyday speech, on the basis of it. Meaning is established in a rough-and-ready, open-textured fashion and is made only as precise as is required by the task at hand—with absolute precision being a will-o'-the-wisp. As a kind of "instant proof" of this point, the reader is invited to offer precise definitions of any three of the terms used in this and preceding sentences—and to consider whether any such definitions were at work as these terms were read.

This reminder is exceedingly important for the question of the meaning of religious language. The general thrust of critical philosophy's attack on God talk has been along the lines of lack of preciseness as related to verifiability. It has, of course, become apparent that even the key terms in this attack, such as "verifiable," "observation," and "relevant," are not definable with absolute precision. Furthermore, the terms employed in order to sharpen up these key definitions are themselves without previous definition, *ad infinitum*. Critical analysis arises out of the matrix of roughhewn ordinary discourse, and so does religious language. This does not imply that those who speak religiously are free to speak as loosely and confusedly as they like, but it does mean that a great deal of caution needs to be invoked when a consideration of the meaning of religious discourse is taken up.[3] The criterion of meaningfulness in religion must be developed in terms of significant, not absolute, precision.

One more word. Given the contextual and functional character of linguistic meaning in general and religious discourse in particular, it would seem imperative that a consideration of the latter needs to begin with and always be grounded in the concrete expressions actually used by those who speak religiously and theologically. Such generally has not been the case. Rather, critical philosophers have indulged themselves in the practice of speaking in general, with only the barest examples, on the nature of religious meaning. The briefest perusal of the literature in this field makes this lack amply clear.[4] The following discussion will seek to bear this requirement in mind, even though this is not the place to present detailed analyses of actual religious usage.

MEDIATION AND METAPHOR

In the light of the foregoing considerations, and especially in view of the account of the structure of religious experience given in Chapter 9, the question of the basic nature of religious discourse can now be faced more directly. Perhaps the single most important characteristic of experience in general and of religious experience in particular which has been suggested is that of their *mediational quality*. The religious dimension of reality is experienced as mediated in and through the other dimensions, and as such is indirect (as distinct from a mystical view) without being inferential (in contrast to a critical view). According to this model of experience, the particulars of the less rich, mediating dimensions are essential yet insufficient to an account of the awareness of the divine. Thus both existentialist and rationalist (whether liberal or orthodox) perspectives, respectively, are transcended.

The main proposal of this chapter is that the mode of speech which is most appropriate to giving expression to mediated experience is the *metaphoric mode*. A brief discussion of the structure of metaphoric speech should make this appropriateness sufficiently clear. Setting aside those interpretations which view metaphor as a translatable substitute for more straightforward expression, one finds it both possible and fruitful to think of metaphor as a mode of speech in which the user calls attention to and/or affirms an aspect of experienced reality that has not been, and perhaps cannot be, captured in more direct speech.[5] Metaphor speaks of the intangible but nonetheless real aspects of human experience. It does this by combining words and phrases from two generally distinguished realms of discourse so as to express an insight about the one *in and through* the other. In a word, metaphor mediates the understanding of a richer dimension of reality by means of locutions characteristic of a less rich dimension.

More specifically, in metaphor a kind of *interaction* is set up between two commonly disassociated language games, shedding light on both, but having a primary *vectorial direction* from the less comprehensive toward the more comprehensive.[6] The dynamic of this vector is provided by a threefold tension between the key words, the different realms of discourse, and the "is and is not" character of the act of predication. The tension generated by this threefold juxtaposition forces the hearer toward an engagement with a richer and more comprehensive perspective; it *mediates* an awareness which transcends the more familiar. To say "War is hell" or "Life is a cabaret" is to illuminate at one and the same time both war and life on the one hand and hell and cabarets on the other hand. Moreover, it is to call attention to, indeed to reveal, a dimension of experienced reality which transcends what was known about the two different dimensions of experience prior to their being brought together in this way.

In a similar vein, to speak of God as father (or mother), ruler, and fortress, or to speak of Christ as advocate, lamb, friend, and brother, is to seek to call attention to a perspective on human life, a dimension of experience, which is both mediated by and yet transcendent of those relationships expressed in the predicates of such statements. Of course, simply to speak in metaphor in general or in religious metaphor in particular is not thereby to guarantee either that the dimension spoken of is real or that the hearer will be able to prehend or grasp it if it is real. The epistemological aspect of religious expression will be treated more fully in the next chapter. Suffice it to say at this juncture that there do need to be, and indeed *are,* functioning criteria for evaluating the efficacy of metaphorical speech as it is employed in religion.

Speaking in a general way, it can be said that those expressions which find a place in the communities and cultures of humankind are properly judged as bearers of meaning. More specifically, those metaphoric expressions around which the languages of the major religions and traditions cluster can be said to have vindicated themselves as meaningful to vast numbers of people throughout the centuries and across cultures. In spite of the many conflicting claims and affirmations of disbelief within and between these different linguistic traditions, there is a strong *prima facie* case for the reality of a religious dimension in the experience of humanity. Not only is there extraordinary agreement of belief in a richer dimension of reality among religious people, but there is also a commonality of linguistic expression in the sense of metaphoric speech.

There is, of course, a strong point of connection between the notion of metaphor and that of analogy. Analogical predication, especially when understood proportionally rather than univocally or equivocally, has basically the same mediational pattern as has been herein ascribed to metaphor.[7] The characteristic being predicated of a richer, more comprehensive dimension via a less rich and narrower dimension is attributed to both dimensions but in ways that are appropriate to each. Moreover, our understanding of the former is in terms of, or comes in and through, our understanding of the latter. The analogy reveals, it is hoped, something that was hither to unnoticed, it *mediates* it.

One other linguistic pattern that relates to the metaphoric mode is that of *paradox*. Whenever two dimensions are brought together in a single utterance, tension will be generated. This is especially true when one dimension is seeking expression in and through the other. Paradox has often been defined as an "apparent but resolvable contradiction," but this is to miss a very important dynamic in paradoxical speech, one that is especially crucial to talk of God. When used mediationally, paradox is neither an apparent contradiction nor an example of nonsense. Rather, it functions as a juncture or intersection for mystery. Often efforts to define or resolve paradoxical utterances can be successful, even illuminating, but with those which function at the deepest level of human existence something essential is generally lost in the process. Divine sovereignty *and* human responsibility, faith *and* works, God's transcendence *and* immanence—utterances that express both sides of these couplets lose their insightfulness when resolved by too much theological footwork.[8]

EVOCATION AND PARABLE

As was mentioned earlier in this chapter, much of the difficulty with respect to questions about the meaningfulness of religious discourse arises because of what J. L. Austin termed "the descriptive fallacy." That is to say, it is nearly always assumed that language in general and God talk in particular have as their primary, if not exclusive, function to *describe* entities and states of affairs. Although the later work of Wittgenstein is generally credited with having demolished this assumption, the fact remains that most of the work in the field of religious language continues to revolve around this issue. The core of the problem is that the usual level of understanding of what constitutes a description is very minimal. This is why it is so essential to introduce and explore the metaphoric mode as a sophisticated form of description in the sense that within it one can speak of intangible dimensions and aspects of experience *in and through* the tangible. This allows for talk about richer, mediated reality beyond sensory observation without trailing off into symbolic "word salad."

It is, of course, the contention of these pages that in the metaphoric mode we are able to transcend simple description without sacrificing cognitivity. There are complex, intangible realities which contribute to the constitution of our world and experience every bit as much as do the facts of physical existence, and these are best expressed in a linguistic mode that is sufficiently rich to embody their mediated character. The moral and aesthetic dimensions of experience are obvious cases in point. The contention here is that religious reality is also of this character. Metaphoric speech, including analogy and paradox, is appropriately structured to express these intangible dimensions, due to its interactionary, mediational pattern. In metaphor we speak about dimensions of reality which are mediated through others with utterances wherein the former is communicated about in and through language about the latter.[9]

Moreover, when we so speak, there often is a cognitive thrust to our utterances. To say, "Communism is a religion" not only makes a claim that enhances our understanding of communism *and* religion but the discussion over the truth or falsity of the claim is both enlightening and meaningful. To say, "The source of creative energy in the world is a personal being" not only casts light both on creativity and on personhood but also makes a claim about the character of the world for which some people find confirming evidence (while others find disconfirming evidence) in their experience. In both cases, there is a claim being made, a cognitive insight being affirmed about a richer, more intangible dimension of life in and through the language appropriated from a more familiar dimension. This is the logic of metaphor, and it befits the structure of mediated experience.

A helpful way of avoiding the descriptive fallacy without relinquishing cognitivity is to speak of the *evocative* force of metaphoric speech. The metaphoric mode seeks to capture and express an insight into a mediated dimension of experience in such a way as to evoke an awareness of this mediated aspect on the part of the hearer. Paul Ricoeur calls this effort at evocation "impertinent predication" because it crosses established categories in a startling and fruitful manner. It is important to note that the claim here is not that metaphoric speech evokes certain feelings or mental pictures in the hearer (which would be a subjectivist approach), but that it actually assists the hearer to see, experience, or understand some aspect of experienced reality differently and/or better.[10] Calling David Thompson "the franchise" of the Denver Nuggets basketball team (a "live" metaphor, as opposed to "the star," a dead metaphor) evokes an understanding of his relationship to the team that exceeds box-score totals, attendance records, etc. Referring to Christ as "the lamb of God" evokes an understanding of his relationship to human experience and evil which goes beyond talk of sacrifice, payment for sin, etc. But the "beyond" can be neither pointed to directly nor defined explicitly.

On the basis of an analysis of a solid cross section of religious discourse, from prayers, creeds, and testimonials to theology and ethical exhortations, it is possible to see the pervasive nature of the metaphoric, mediational pattern.[11] There is a decided, twofold, *couplet structure* to much religious language that bears witness to the mediational character of metaphoric speech by refusing either to reduce it to straightforward description on the one hand or to sever it entirely from cognitivity concerns on the other hand. In spite of scholarly critiques (especially those following Bultmann) which separate religious insight and expression from the factual and cognitive dimension, it remains the case that the New Testament accounts are replete with factual and cognitive details. Indeed, the message is inextricably embedded in these details. At the same time, however, it must be acknowledged that the spiritual insights and claims of the New Testament go beyond mere facts and details as well. It seems apparent that in this case, as with almost all others in human experience, the former are mediated in and through the latter, both in speech and in experienced reality.

More specifically, when Biblical, creedal, and theological writers speak of God and the divine dimension, they frequently express themselves according to a twofold, metaphoric pattern. Consider such *Biblical expressions* as "heavenly Father," "Lord of glory," "the bread of life," "living water," "born again," and the like. This frequent coupling of a term taken from a more straightforward, physical dimension of life with another term (such as "heavenly," "glory," "life") that functions as a *modifier* bespeaks of a metaphorical pattern. Unfortunately traditional interpretations of Biblical language (both pro and con) have taken these modifiers as descriptive terms and have thus divested the expressions of their evocative power. I would suggest, rather, that they be viewed as *reminders* that while the reality being spoken of is grounded in and mediated through the particulars of everyday experience, it also transcends those particulars. They function more as operators in an equation (such as " $=$ " or " $+$ ") than as variables (such as "2" or "¼").

The same sort of twofold pattern can be seen in *theological language,* both in negative characterizations (e.g., "God is immutable") and in positive attributions (e.g., "God is pure being"). In a great number of cases the predication is qualified by another term which serves to indicate that the statement functions metaphorically. Many famous (and infamous!) theological disputes can be fruitfully understood as efforts to bring religious reality to expression without giving way either to flat literalism or empty symbolism. The reality of both the immediate and the mediated must be preserved if the evocative thrust of the metaphoric mode is to be preserved.

Another way of viewing the metaphoric mode as a bearer of religious meaning is in terms of the *parable* or story.[12] Parables can be thought of as extended metaphors, for they are to be distinguished from both factual accounts and allegories. In a parable an insight or claim about spiritual reality is *embodied* in the details of a story set in familiar circumstances. While the point of the story cannot be equated with those details, neither can it be communicated apart from them. The single thrust of the parable is best said to be mediated *in and through* the details. Moreover, in the giving of a parable, as with all metaphoric speech, room is provided for the hearer to have both the opportunity of apprehending and responding to the truth *and* the responsibility of so doing. The hearer is confronted, challenged, and set free by the metaphoric mode because it is an *indirect* form of communication, as befits mediated dimensions in general and spiritual reality in particular.

PERFORMANCE AND DIALOGUE

Another major source of critical confusion in the field of religious discourse is a failure to distinguish between the sort of God talk engaged in by religious persons *as such* (a first-order activity) and that generated by religious theorizers who talk *about* religion and religious discourse (a second-order activity). At a rough-and-ready level it is helpful to make an initial distinction between these two, designating the former the "religious use of language" and the latter "theological language." Much of the foregoing discussion has centered around theological language and it is now time to explore some different aspects of religious language. Although some of what has already been said pertains to the religious use of language as well as to the theological use, there are significant features of the former which bear closer consideration, especially within a post-critical context.

As was mentioned earlier, the primary function of language, whether in theological or religious use, is *not* descriptive. Descriptions in general and descriptions of God and/or of the religious dimension in particular do not stand alone; they are not made for their own sake. The vast majority of religious uses of language aim at accomplishing some concrete task within the religious life itself. Thus (1) believers participate in corporate and personal worship, (2) they speak to one another in order to understand and edify in the faith, and (3) they speak with nonbelievers by way of sharing their faith with them. There are common elements of performance and dialogue within each of these religious uses of language and I should like to explore them briefly before bringing this chapter to a close.

J. L. Austin has called attention to what he termed the "performative" function of language.[13] It will suffice for our present purposes simply to indicate that he pointed out that in certain linguistic situations we not only *say* certain things, but we *do* certain things *by* making the statement as well. When we say "I'm sorry," for instance, in addition to speaking we *perform* the *act* of apologizing. In like manner, when we say "I promise," "I consent," and "I warn you" (as well as "Strike three," "We find the defendant guilty," and "Please pass the salad"), we engage in performative utterances. At first Austin contrasted such uses with descriptive uses ("constatives"), but eventually he came to stress the multidimensional nature of all language and accordingly sought to overcome the cognitive/noncognitive dichotomy. This makes him an ally of post-critical thought.[14]

A certain amount of work has been done to bring Austin's insights to bear on religious language,[15] but I shall not seek to review it here. The main area of concern has been that of liturgical and/or sacramental speech within the context of corporate worship. Baptism, confession, absolution, and benediction all exhibit performative characteristics. Moreover, even creed-saying, hymn-singing, and tithing can be profitably understood in this way. Incidentally, it is more than just interesting to note how the Old Testament stresses the creative power of God as embodied in speech: "And God said, 'Let there be light'"; "Hear, O Israel: The LORD our God is one LORD"; and "The word of the LORD came to me." Likewise the New Testament stresses Christ as the divine Word. There is a performative element involved here as well, in that reality is altered through the linguistic act.

Dialogue, too, plays an important role in the religious use of language. It will be recalled that a post-critical understanding of both experience and language was seen to focus on the cruciality of relationship as the primary category of human existence. Sharedness and reciprocity are an essential part of the fabric or matrix comprising our lives, even in relation to our interaction with the physical dimension. Furthermore, these qualities are especially significant in highly mediated dimensions of experience, such as the religious. Thus, when one discusses the character of God talk it is imperative to give some place to its dialogical nature. Two aspects of dialogue as it pertains to the religious use of language bear special mention.

First, there is the dialogue between and among human beings. Within the believing community people speak to one another religiously in order to come to deeper understanding and build one another up in the faith. It is in and through this give-and-take that the reality of the religious dimension is mediated. Language as a dialogical process in, around, and about a shared experience of the divine both helps constitute and gives expression to religious experience. Only against the backdrop of this dialogical understanding of the nature of speech can God talk be appreciated. In a similar vein, but with a wider scope, is the nature of believers' linguistic exchanges with nonbelievers about religion to be understood. The purpose is to find common aspects of mutually experienced dimensions of reality and to explore those in such a way as to help bring about an awareness of a yet more comprehensive and rich dimension. To return to the themes of the last section of this chapter, through dialogue the believer seeks to evoke a shared experience with the nonbeliever. Moreover, if the dialogue is authentic, the believer may well learn a good deal from the interaction as well.

Second, there is the mysterious, asymmetrical dialogue involved when people speak, not *about* God, but *to* God. Generally, of course, such uses of language are classified as prayer. Although there is a myriad of material on prayer, there is almost nothing by way of exploring its philosophical ramifications as a linguistic phenomenon.[16] Of course, an important feature of the prayers given in corporate worship, as well as those published in books and magazines, is their social or human effect. Such prayers are spoken at least partly for the benefit of other human beings. It is private or personal prayer which stands as an anomaly, for it is a kind of one-sided dialogue.

In addition to all the helpful things that can be pointed out about the autosuggestive efficacy of speaking to God privately, it remains the case that the vast majority of those who pray would contend that far more than this is involved. Space will permit our noting only a single important feature of this form of God talk, which might serve as a fruitful point of departure for further exploration. As with language in general, so with prayer, those of us who participate in it in a sense simply *find ourselves doing so* without being able to say precisely why. There is a certain bedrock quality about all forms of linguistic activity, including speaking to God. We speak not only *in order* to be understood but also *because* we are understood. For the believer, prayer is no more optional—or even voluntary—than is language for all humans. Prayer, like language, takes place, and we find ourselves involved in it. The standard question of whether or not private prayer is wasted effort since there may be no hearer raises epistemological issues which are best treated in the next chapter. From a linguistic point of view, all forms of speech would seem to carry with them some form of reciprocity; otherwise they would not persist within human experience. More work needs to be done here.

11

RELIGIOUS KNOWLEDGE

This chapter is meant to provide the culmination of the main argument animating the book as a whole. I began (Part One) by identifying, analyzing, and critiquing critical philosophy, focusing on the crucial concepts of experience, meaning, and knowledge. Keeping these same concepts at the center, I then moved to an introduction and exploration of a post-critical posture (Part Two). Up to this point the explicit theme was the contrast between critical and post-critical thought, with emphasis given to the superiority of the latter. The implicit theme was the possibility that "the heart has reasons which reason knows not of."

Beginning with the last two chapters (Part Three), I have sought to bring post-critical insights to bear directly on religious epistemology. Thus the question of the viability of the notion of "reasons of the heart" has become increasingly prominent. In the present chapter this question arrives at the center of the stage. Against the backdrop provided by the foregoing investigations, it should now be possible to state the case for reasons of the heart in relation to the issue of religious knowing. The specific concern of the present chapter is a post-critical justification of religious belief. The aim will be to clarify how there can and must be knowledge based on reasons which are nonetheless rational for lying "beneath" the explicit reasoning process.

Proof and Justification

Aristotle once said that it is foolish to expect a different sort of rigor within a given area of concern than is appropriate to it. When applied to the question of religious knowledge this insight has enormously important consequences. The major flaw in critical philosophy is to seek the rigor appropriate to an axiomatic system, whether mathematical or Newtonian, with respect to areas of experience where it is inappropriate. The tight, wholly explicit concept of justification of belief focused in the requirement of logicoscientific proof has a very narrow range of application indeed. It needs to be replaced by (in fact, it needs justification itself in terms of) a broader concept of *confirmation*.

One way of pinpointing this need is the following. In critical thought three criteria are suggested for judging whether or not knowledge obtains: (1) the person must believe that such and such is the case, (2) the person must have good reasons for so believing, and (3) such and such must, in fact, *be* the case. Only when all three of these criteria are met is the person justified in claiming to *know*. Aside from the difficulties inherent in defining any such criteria (*any* person? what is meant by "believe," "good reasons," and "in fact"?), it is clear that such a narrow view of knowledge is inflationary, since it leaves most of us with very little knowledge, indeed. Moreover, it is circular in that the third criterion uses the notion of *knowing* that such and such is the case; how can the criteria for what constitutes knowing that such and such is the case include knowing that it is, in fact, the case?

A post-critical understanding of the justification of belief limits itself to the first two criteria mentioned above. If a person believes that such and such is the case and has good reason to so believe, he or she is justified in that belief and can lay a claim to having knowledge. "Good reasons" does *not* mean an airtight case, but it does imply that within the context in question the reasons carry the relevant persons "beyond a reasonable doubt." Nor does this concept of justification imply that the belief cannot turn out to be wrong. All that is claimed here is that if the two criteria are fulfilled, the person is entitled to *say* that he or she *knows*. Even the claim that the original belief "turned out to be wrong" is itself a belief that can be justified only by good reasons, not by "proof."[1]

Thus when believers say they believe in God (in the sense of believing *that* such a being exists) or that "God was in Christ," this belief is justified if (1) they do manifest, both in word *and* deed (i.e., not superficially), that they so believe and if (2) they can give good reasons for so believing. While the notion of "good reasons" is not to be equated with proof, it is also clear that it must carry us past such moves as "Because it's comforting," or "Because I might be punished if I don't." There will, of course, be differences of opinion about borderline cases, just as there will not always be agreement about who was at fault in an argument or whether or not this person loves that person. Such difficulties do not, however, obviate the possibility of a believer's claim to religious knowledge in a given case.

A helpful way of developing the idea of the justification of religious belief is along the lines of what might be termed *experiential "adequacy"* or "fit."[2] A religious belief is both vast and deep in its implications. Therefore it cannot be treated as a single hypothesis or even as a full-blown theory. In many ways, because of its great profundity and comprehensiveness, it can be said to bring with it its own criteria. And yet, people do come to accept or take on religious beliefs (as well as rejecting and dropping them), so they are not to be conceived of as self-contained systems of thought. The sort of confirmation appropriate to such types of belief is necessarily flexible and contextual; that is, it must be grounded in experience and relative to the persons involved. Moreover, no hard-and-fast criteria and procedures for determining the degree of justification of the belief can be devised in advance. There are, to be sure, certain guidelines that can be employed to ensure against gullibility, self-deception, and propagandizing.

One such guideline is that of *comprehensive coherence.* An adequate or fitting belief is one that relates in a unifying and consistent fashion to other beliefs within the broad and important dimensions of human existence. Such coherence will never be complete or exhaustive, of course. Nevertheless, one's religious convictions should make sense out of and/or shed light upon life's major questions about reality, truth, and value. The particular way in which religious belief does this within the life of an individual or community is, to be sure, a complex matter and deserves examination. Such exploration and dialogue are themselves part of the application of the guideline under discussion. Given the limitations of human existence, comprehensive coherence is something to be sought, not ensured.

A second helpful guideline might be termed *internal consistency.* Here the idea is that the religious belief in question must be harmonious, both in relation to itself (not self-contradictory) and with respect to other beliefs within the person's overall religious commitment. Once again, because of the nature of human experience and thought, absolute consistency is neither possible nor necessary. Nonetheless, effort should be made to guard against adopting a belief or set of beliefs which is internally inconsistent. To be sure, it is frequently impossible to determine whether or not beliefs are absolutely consistent. Some questions will need to be "tabled" until a later time, the best that one can hope for is "rough-and-ready" consistency, and some issues will never be settled at all. Moreover, care must be taken not to make hasty judgments about apparently inconsistent beliefs. Paradoxes are sometimes resolvable—and sometimes they bear witness to deep mysteries which are revealing of truth even though they remain "unsolvable."

A third guideline might be called *ethical fruitfulness*. In addition to making sense out of and shedding light on the important concerns of human existence, an experientially adequate religious belief should make a strong contribution to the person's moral development and integrity. This guideline might be thought of as a pragmatic one, since its emphasis is on personal character and effectiveness. In spite of the fact that morality and growth are extremely complex and relative notions, it is both necessary and possible for sound judgments to be made about them. A great deal of empathetic care and exploration are required when one is aiming at such judgments, and in the final analysis each person will have to be his or her own judge. Nevertheless, there are certain shared "absolutes" among humankind which must be and are invoked every day and in every culture. I have in mind such standards as the value of life, happiness, loyalty, and truth.

It is sometimes claimed that religious belief precludes the possibility of ever admitting that one is wrong, of any experience or argument ever counting decisively against the belief. Even though believers as well as nonbelievers sometimes take this point of view, it seems to me completely wrongheaded. It is true that if a religious belief is worth holding, and if it is held with real commitment, there will be a tendency to affirm it against negative evidence. Nonetheless, to hold a belief is to claim that it is true, and if a belief is true, it is logically possible that it can also be false. Thus to contend that a religious belief is beyond being false is tantamount to contending that it is beyond being true as well. A responsible religious commitment is one wherein the person remains open to further experience, even though it is not necessary to state beforehand precisely at what point one would withdraw his or her commitment. Nor need the quality and degree of one's commitment depend upon and fluctuate with the absoluteness of that which is believed. Adequacy, not certainty, is what makes belief responsible.

PARTICIPATION AND COMMUNITY

As was argued in Chapter 7, all forms of knowing require the participation of the knower. Knowing is a relational experience and thus the person who desires to know must in some way *engage* the dimension or aspect of reality which serves as the object of interest. Nor can this engagement be merely a passive sort of observation. Although on a surface level it is important to speak of "disinterested examination" in the name of "objectivity," at a more fundamental level it is clear that only on the basis of active engagement can knowing take place at all. Furthermore, such involvement is dependent, as well, on the development of skills and judgment, both of which require the personal commitment of the knower *as* knower.

In religious knowledge we should not expect things to be different. Although it seems ludicrous on the face of it, it must be admitted that the majority of philosophers propounding theories about religion in general and religious knowledge in particular not only come to negative conclusions, but *disclaim* any religious involvement whatsoever. It is not out of place to suggest that they come to the conclusions they do *because* of their lack of involvement. Just as it would be absurd for a philosopher to theorize about science or art without some firsthand experience of those dimensions of reality, so too it seems absurd for thinkers who are not in some way participants in the religious dimension of life to pass judgment on its meaning and viability. This is especially true if religion is to be thought of in terms of personal and relational characteristics.

A special feature of the interpretation of knowledge being proposed on these pages is that it centers in the notion of the *integrative act* as opposed to that of the inferential process. Contrary to critical philosophy's assumption that knowledge is dependent on and is obtained by analysis of particulars, the point of departure for post-critical thought is the act of grasping the whole as an intelligible and comprehensive entity. This act *integrates* hitherto disrelated particulars into a gestalt, not by a process of accumulated observation and inference, but by a participatory dynamic of interrelationship which seeks and intends meaning. Such holistic-oriented activity provides the context within and basis upon which knowledge by analysis and inference can take place.

Thus it is that religious knowledge, understood post-critically, must be disassociated from the notions of inference, whether deductive or inductive. Whatever else they might do, the classic "proofs" of God's existence, for instance, do not provide religious knowledge. Nor does the accumulation of data from various fields—such as archaeology, psychology, physics, and history—establish an epistemological basis for an inductive inference about the truth of religion. Any and all of these factors, and others besides them, may, however, function as a kind of *catalyst* or *juncture point* for the integration of a whole host of particulars into a single insight or perspective that will serve as the basis of religious epistemological claims.

Christians, for instance, claim that the deeds and sayings of Jesus provide a fulcrum point from which it is possible to relate to and participate in life and the world most meaningfully. Religious knowledge may at some points involve inferential processes, but they do not provide the point of departure. Nor is this beginning point, therefore, provided by a "leap of faith." Rather, the mediational character of dimensional reality, together with the dynamics of tacit knowing, serves as the experiential matrix within which the deeds and words of Jesus operate as the integrative factor. Once the integration takes place, religious knowing can be said to be at work. We shall return to this pattern in the next section.

It is, of course, crucial to bear in mind that the participatory aspect of religious knowing is not individualistic in nature. Rather, it takes place within a historic and contemporary *community*. Indeed, one important dimension of the participatory aspect is the social. Religious reality must not be thought of as mediated exclusively to the individual, but as coming in and through the social dimension in general and the religious community in particular. In fact, participation itself implies the active presence of other persons, living and working together. It is within and by means of the current community that religious knowing is awakened, explored, and confirmed. There is here a symbiotic relationship between the (any) individual knower and the community—each exists and is defined in terms of the other, both are necessary to religious knowing as a phenomenon. Through sharing, confrontation, and struggle, differences are resolved and growth ensues in dialectical fashion.

The record of this ongoing dialectic constitutes the historic dimension of community, frequently referred to as the *tradition*. Not only does religious knowing take place in relation to other persons in current experience, but it exists in relation to those who have participated in and helped define the community in the past. The divine is mediated through history as well as through nature and other living persons. It is naive for a person to think that he or she stands alone in his or her discernment of the religious dimension. Without a tradition there would be no such awareness. Thus there is a sense in which the thoughts and actions of those who have preceded us must function authoritatively in the present. Since knowing is a dialogue, this authority is not absolute, but the burden of proof lies with the person who would deviate from the tradition. Once again there is a symbiotic relationship between tradition and current, individual insight and need. Each needs and defines the other.[3]

The Tacit and the Contextual

Within the general parameters provided by the foregoing sections, it is now possible to zero in more directly on the specific structure of religious knowing. I want to draw heavily on the discussions in Chapter 7 wherein the tacit foundations of all knowing were affirmed and explored. Specifically, I shall suggest that it is especially helpful to think of religious knowledge as primarily tacit in character. That is to say, the particular events, concepts, and beliefs that are generally thought to constitute religious knowledge are themselves only mediators of a richer, more comprehensive dimension of reality which cannot be explicitly designated. Moreover, these particulars themselves only take on their religious significance from within the context or perspective provided by the broader and richer, but essentially tacit dimension.

The following diagram may serve well to summarize the distinctions and emphases developed earlier which pertain to tacit knowing. The awareness dimension of experience moves from its subsidiary pole toward the focal, while the activity dimension flows from its bodily pole toward the conceptual. The interaction of focal awareness and conceptual activity gives rise to *explicit knowing,* while the interaction between subsidiary awareness and bodily activity gives rise to *tacit knowing.* Together these form the poles of the cognitivity dimension of experience. Awareness and activity are simultaneous and experientially dialectical in relation to one another. The latter is not a response to the former. More important, the vectorial thrust of both of these dimensions renders tacit knowing *logically prior,* though not experientially prior, to explicit knowing. All explicit knowing is grounded in tacit knowing and not all tacit knowing can be made explicit.

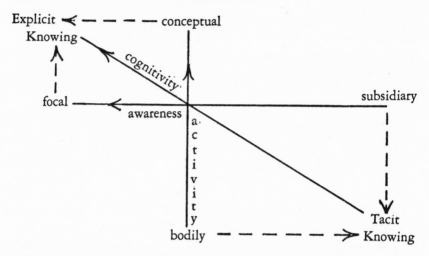

Two important issues arise in connection with the application of this epistemological model to the question of religious knowledge. The first concerns the actual experiential pattern of religious knowing vis-à-vis the awareness and activity dimensions. The second pertains to the justification of the claim to religious knowledge. In both cases the concept of mediation is crucial. Religious knowledge arises in and through other dimensions and aspects of experience, and it is justified on the basis of considerations which lie beneath explicit justificatory processes. Let us look more closely at each of these concerns.

Incidentally, it seems appropriate that a highly mediated dimension of experience such as the religious would yield knowledge that is primarily tacit in character. That which is experienced in and through other dimensions cannot itself be focused explicitly, either in terms of specific concepts and propositions or in terms of its cognitive basis. This does *not* mean, however, that no responsible rationale can (and must) be developed. The one that is developed must be contiguous with a mediationally structured experience. In like manner, it is appropriate that mediated and tacit experiential knowledge will find its primary mode of expression to be metaphoric, since it allows for more being known than can be said directly. The overarching theme of the post-critical approach that is presented in these pages is the interwoven character of the concepts of the mediated, the tacit, and the metaphoric.

With respect to the experiential pattern of religious knowing, I suggest that it is helpful to think of the divine dimension being mediated to us, of our becoming aware of it, subsidiarily. In and through the events, persons, activities, and ideas with which we have to do in our historical, social, and personal experience we become subsidiarily aware of a dimension which unifies and enriches these particulars. At the same time, in and through our interaction with each and all of these particulars we give expression to work out our commitments and values. The conjunction and interweaving of these two dimensions creates the experiential matrix out of which our most fundamental knowledge is formed. This tacit fabric, in turn, provides the context within which our explicit ideas and decisions take shape.

To put this dynamic in theological language, God's self-revelation is mediated to us, both through nature, society, and conscience on the one hand and through historical event and record on the other hand, in and through the various dimensions of our lives. We become subsidiarily aware of this revelation. At the same time, by our involvements, commitments, reasonings, and decisions we embody our interaction with our subsidiary awareness of God's active revelation in our lives. This symbiotic dialectic forms the firm, but tacit, basis of religious faith out of which flow the more explicit conceptual and behavioral expressions of religious knowledge. It is this tacit dimension of our experience which gives rise to the cognitive aspect of religious awareness. It is thus neither "blind faith" nor strict inferential validation. Faith and revelation meet one another at the juncturing of action and mediated (subsidiary) self-disclosure, and together they form religious knowing.

All of this does not deny the explicit nature and function of such factors as the Judeo-Christian tradition, the historical events of the exodus and the incarnation, personal and institutional witness, etc. It simply seeks to place such factors in their proper perspective epistemologically. They do *not* constitute proofs or data from which our knowledge of God's activity in the world, our awareness of the divine dimension, can be inferred. Rather, they function as the particulars within the various dimensions of experienced reality *through* which God can be said to be revealed. They are the glass through which we see God, albeit darkly—and sufficiently.

With respect to the rational justification of the above experiential dynamic, i.e., the manner in which tacit knowing can be justified as a whole, a number of things have already been said in sections 1 and 2 of the present chapter. In a more formal vein, it remains to be pointed out once again that *all* justification is in fact contextual, that there is no such thing as absolute or ultimate justification of any belief, position, or framework. All justification must come to an end somewhere, just as all inference must begin somewhere—and these terminal points cannot themselves be justified by any formal, explicit procedure. In a word, all knowledge has an informal or tacit base. Thus it is not ostrich-headed to affirm the tacit character of religious knowing. Such a move does not vindicate all epistemological claims, for there remains the necessity of informal validation even of claims to tacit knowing. Some of the patterns of this sort of process were discussed in the first half of the present chapter.

Perhaps the most forceful and pointed formulation of the contextual and tacit character of all justificatory processes at the foundational level is that found in the work (1931) of Kurt Gödel.[4] Gödel developed his "proof" in highly specialized mathematical language and it was aimed specifically at the justification of self-contained, logical systems. Nevertheless, it has broader application and its general point is fairly easy to grasp. The proof is generally acknowledged to be incontestable by mathematicians and logicians. In brief, Gödel demonstrated that no system of thought is self-contained, since it must draw upon reasoning processes which lie outside the system itself in order to establish its own consistency. Thus the question of the justification of a system of thought or a rational process, a question that can be raised within that system or process, can only be answered by an appeal to reasoning not contained therein. In a word, all formal and explicit concepts and inferences stand in need of, and are based on, informal and tacit acts of integration which can never be formalized without simply repeating the same problem.

Thus the justification of claims to knowledge must and can only be based in informal and tacit reasoning within the parameters supplied by the context. Although these informal reasoning processes cannot be fully articulated and explicitly demonstrated, they can be and are vindicated daily in the way we live.[5] Religious knowledge claims are no exception. Because they pertain to the richest and most comprehensive dimension of experienced reality as mediated through the other dimensions, it is understandable that no explicit justification can be given of them. They, too, must show themselves in the pragmatic efficacy of everyday living. In the final analysis, all knowing must be *embodied* in order to be justified.

CONFIDENCE AND HUMILITY

Two corollaries of the above position need to be clarified. The first is that obviously there is no guarantee that any or all claims to religious knowledge are true. To interpret the structure of religious awareness as mediated dimensionally does not entail either that everyone *is* aware of the divine dimension or that all those who *claim* to be interacting with religious reality are in fact doing so. All that can be done here is to sketch out the structure of *possible* religious knowing—the actuality of such knowledge is not a philosophical matter but is an existential one. This brings us to the second corollary—namely, that in the final analysis the vindication of religious knowledge claims, since they are mediated and tacit in character, will have to take place in the give-and-take of everyday life, in the interaction between and among persons on both the personal and the social level. The quality and human efficacy of commitments and life-styles is the ultimate criterion for judging whether or not the divine is being engaged. Such judgments are, to be sure, exceedingly difficult to make—but they are neither avoidable nor impossible. "You will know them by their fruits."

The post-critical posture toward the possibility of religious knowledge as outlined above yields both confidence and humility. The *confidence* derives from the fact that a post-critical understanding of understanding frees the knowing agent to make a twofold affirmation. First, it is now possible to affirm the fundamental values which render the quest for knowledge possible—namely, that there is a world to be known and that it can be known. To raise doubts about these possibilities, as does critical philosophy, not only is self-stultifying but it is self-contradictory as well, since even rational doubt is parasitic on them. As human beings participating in life we are already embarked as knowing agents and are not given the luxury of detachment. To pretend that such detachment is possible, or even that it would be helpful, is simply to engage in self-deception.

According to post-critical thought, we can and must affirm the world and our knowledge of it as we interact with it and seek to know it—even when and as we fail in such efforts. Religious epistemology also participates in this confidence by affirming the reality and knowability of the divine as experienced in and through the other dimensions of human life. In a fundamental sense the burden of proof has been shifted to those who would begin by denying such possibilities, since religious experience and tradition are already on the scene when critical philosophy arises. It is not possible to wipe the slate clean, so the case must be made for abandoning religious knowledge rather than for acknowledging it.

Secondly, a post-critical posture allows the knowing agent to accredit his or her ability to make *judgments and commitments* within the framework provided by the above structural affirmation. With the insight that knowledge does not exist in the abstract, that every claim to know must be made by some person as a knowing agent, comes the confidence—as well as the responsibility—to make such judgments. All knowledge is the result of human concern, effort, and sharing and can occur only when persons and communities accredit their own powers to seek and obtain knowledge. Critical philosophy undercuts this confidence by defining knowledge in impersonal terms and by assuming that all knowledge claims are false until proven true.

Here, too, we can see that religious epistemology profits from the post-critical perspective. Cognitive confidence with respect to experience of the divine is based in the acritical belief that if there is a God, humans can know it, can interact with the divine reality. Even though there in no guarantee that each or any particular claim to religious knowledge is reliable, the fundamental possibility that one or some *can* be reliable may and must be affirmed. Once again, personal involvement in the search for such knowledge is a necessary condition for achieving it—unless we accredit our own judgments and commitments in *principle*, we can never experience the divine. Such reasoning does not obviate the necessity of divine initiative and self-disclosure, it only stresses the parallel necessity of human involvement.

The confidence being urged in the above paragraphs may well be summarized in the notion of "universal intent" developed by Michael Polanyi.[6] The structure and patterns of the human way of being-in-the-world exhibit a pivotal cognitive dimension wherein explicit knowing flows out of tacit knowing. We find ourselves as knowing beings and we are unable to justify or fully explain all and why we know. Moreover, in all our cognitive activity we act as if knowledge is both possible and actual—even doubt and skepticism are construed as knowledge-seeking moves. In a word, we *intend* truth, i.e., we aim at it and thereby affirm its existence and our ability to achieve it, at least some of the time. Furthermore, we intend truth *universally* in the sense that we expect others to agree with us when we find and/or express it. Whenever we claim to know anything (even that no truth exists!), we expect others to accept this as true as well. If we say x may be true for you, but not for us (or vice versa), we still expect the other person to accept this overall proposition about the relativity of truth as true for *both* of us—as a universal truth.

Universal intent applies as well to claims to religious knowledge. It is not possible to assert consistently that no truth can be known about religion, or that all claims to religious knowledge are equally valid. Whatever we affirm about the religious dimension of human experience, in the act of affirmation we also affirm that knowledge of the divine is possible (even if only as negative knowledge) and that we know something about it that others ought to agree with. Once again, this insight in no way vindicates any or all individual religious claims, but it does render viable the whole question of religious knowledge.

The *humility* yielded by a post-critical approach to religious epistemology is the other side of the coin from the confidence discussed above. Along with the affirmations inherent within a knowledge claim must also go the implicit acknowledgment that *all* claims to knowledge are subject to error and/or revision. Because knowing is a process entered into by persons and in community, with all the limitations thereunto pertaining, no epistemological claim can be viewed as incorrigible. The continual growth and discovery of the individual and of the community serve both as goad and corrective in the search for knowledge. Even though our claims to knowledge can and must be affirmed with confidence, such affirmations also imply that our claims are open to criticism and correction. For that is what it means to assert a claim in the public arena of language and life. Thus humility is also a vital dimension of knowledge-seeking.

This is no less true with respect to religious knowledge claims. We see through a glass, darkly. No one can claim to speak for God or to have the final word on the divine dimension without thereby obviating the very processes by and through which such claims are made. A human assertion that is not open to criticism and correction places itself beyond the possibility of truth as well. For whereas the universal intent serves as a check against skepticism and relativism, self-corrective humility serves as a guard against self-authentication and arrogance. To confuse a human understanding of the truth with the truth itself is to pretend to be God. Since divine revelation and the experience of the religious are always mediated in character, all claims to knowledge about them are subject to interpretation and modification. Even claims to direct visions are, in the final analysis, *claims* which have to be evaluated and confirmed in the lives of the relevant persons and community. Moreover, all claims must also acknowledge the possibility and the right of others to disagree.

If I believe in God (am convinced of God) in a pluralistic world, a world in which I know there are men of good will who do not so believe, then my faith, if justified at all, must be a faith which takes account of that very pluralism which in part denies my faith. It must be faith justifiable (I must be justified by my faith?) in a world which includes unfaith. Conversely, if I disbelieve, believe in no God, am convinced no God exists, in a world in which I know there are men who do so believe, then my conviction, if justified at all, must be one which takes account of that fact—it must be atheism in a world which includes faith. The pluralism which we envisage, then, does not obviate justification nor require narrowness of outlook, but it does require that the pluralism itself shall be internalized, so that it becomes a factor which my convictions take into account.[7]

NOTES

Chapter 1. THE PACKAGING OF EXPERIENCE

1. Stephen Pepper, *World Hypotheses* (University of California Press, 1942).

2. Immanuel Kant, *Critique of Pure Reason*, tr. by Norman Kemp Smith (St. Martin's Press, 1969), p. 65.

3. Ibid., p. 274:

   "When, therefore, we say that the senses represent objects *as they appear*, and the understanding objects *as they are*, the latter statement is to be taken, not in the transcendental, but in the merely empirical meaning of the terms, namely as meaning that the objects must be represented as objects of experience, that is, as appearances in thorough-going interconnection with one another, and not as they may be apart from their relation to possible experience (and consequently to any senses,) as objects of the pure understanding."

4. René Descartes, *Discourse on Method*, tr. by John Veitch, in *The Rationalists* (Doubleday & Co., n.d.), p. 51:

   "The *second*, to divide each of the difficulties under examination into as many parts as possible, and as might be necessary, for its adequate solution. The *third*, to conduct my thoughts in such order that, by commencing with objects the simplest and easiest to know, I might ascend by little and little, and, as it were, step by step, to the knowledge of the more complex; assigning in thought a certain order even to those objects which in their own nature do not stand in a relation of antecedence and sequence. And the *last*, in every case to make enumerations so complete and reviews so general, that I might be assured that nothing was omitted."

5. David Hume, *A Treatise of Human Nature*, 2d ed., ed. by L. A. Selby-Bigge (Oxford: Clarendon Press, 1967). Hume never offers the slightest apologetic for starting right out explaining human nature by giving an account of "perceptions." In his Introduction he describes his plan aptly: "To march up directly to the capitol or center of these sciences, to human nature itself." Evidently "directly" means "analytically."

6. Kant, *Critique of Pure Reason*, footnote 1.

7. Bertrand Russell, *Principles of Mathematics*, 2d ed. (London, 1927), p. 466:

155

"In every case of analysis, there is a whole consisting of parts with relations; it is only the nature of the parts and the relations which distinguishes different cases."

8. Technically speaking, the early Ayer (Alfred J. Ayer, *Language, Truth and Logic*; London, Oxford University Press, 1936) only wanted philosophers to talk about the *language* of experience, not experience itself. Later on he came around to being more of an advocate of sense-data theory (*The Problem of Knowledge*).

9. Ludwig Wittgenstein, *Tractatus Logico-Philosophicus* (London: Routledge & Kegan Paul, 1961), p. 63:

"If an elementary proposition is true, the state of affairs exists: if an elementary proposition is false, the state of affairs does not exist.

"If all true elementary propositions are listed, the world is completely described. A complete description of the world is given by listing all elementary propositions, and then listing which of them are true and which false."

10. *The Rationalists*, pp. 113-114.

11. Hume, *A Treatise of Human Nature*, p. 1:

"All the perceptions of the human mind resolve themselves into two distinct kinds, which I shall call *Impressions* and *Ideas*. The difference betwixt these consists in the degrees of force and liveliness with which they strike upon the mind, and make their way into our thought or consciousness."

12. Ayer, *Language, Truth and Logic*, pp. 63-65.

13. Bertrand Russell, *Logic and Knowledge* (London: George Allen & Unwin, 1956).

14. Bertrand Russell, *The Problems of Philosophy* (Oxford: Basil Blackwell Publishers, 1970), pp. 3-4:

"Thus it becomes evident that the real table, if there is one, is not the same as what we immediately experience by sight or touch or hearing. The real table, if there is one, is not *immediately* known to us at all, but must be an inference from what is immediately known."

15. Generally the passages quoted and referred to in the notes of the previous sections clearly illustrate these two characteristics as well.

16. Wittgenstein, *Tractatus Logico-Philosophicus*, pp. 15-16.

17. Kant is extremely representative of this point of view. *Critique of Pure Reason*, p. 528:

"Now I maintain that all attempts to employ reason in theology in any merely speculative manner are altogether fruitless and by their very nature null and void, and that the principles of its employment in the study of nature do not lead to any theology whatsoever. Consequently, the only theology of reason which is possible is that which is based upon moral laws or seeks guidance from them. All synthetic principles of reason allow only of an immanent employment; and in order to have knowledge of a supreme being we should have to put them to a transcendent use, for which our understanding is in no way fitted."

18. For a more detailed consideration of how this works itself out in Wittgenstein's thought, cf. my "Wittgenstein and Metaphor," *Philosophy and Phenomenological Research,* Fall 1980.

Chapter 2. LANGUAGE AS REPRESENTATION

1. Plato, *The Sophist* (259d-264b).
2. Aristotle, *Metaphysics,* Book V.
3. Augustine, *Confessions,* Book I.
4. Thomas Aquinas, *Summa Contra Gentiles,* Book I, chs. 30-36.
5. Descartes's whole treatment of ideas presupposes that words name ideas; e.g., *The Rationalists:*
    "Of my thoughts some are, as it were, images of things and to these alone, properly belongs the name idea" (p. 130). "By the name God, I understand a substance infinite." (p. 137).
6. Hume, *A Treatise of Human Nature,* p. 16:
    "The idea of a substance as well as that of a mode is nothing but a collection of simple ideas that are united by the imagination, and have a peculiar *name* assigned them" (italics added).
7. Kant's approach to ideas and concepts reveals a reliance on a naming theory of words, for he continually assigns terms to them with the formula: "This I *entitle* . . . ."
8. Bishop Berkeley, in *The Empiricists* (Doubleday & Co., n.d.), pp. 147-148.
9. Victor Kraft, *The Vienna Circle* (Philosophical Library, 1953).
10. Russell, *The Problems of Philosophy,* p. 53:
    "When we examine common words, we find that, broadly speaking, proper names stand for particulars, while other substantives, adjectives, prepositions, and verbs stand for universals. Pronouns stand for particulars, but are ambiguous: it is only by the context or the circumstances that we know what particulars they stand for. The word 'now' stands for a particular, namely the present moment; but like pronouns, it stands for an ambiguous particular, because the present is always changing."
11. Although strictly speaking Ayer deals with "propositions" rather than with words and names, his analysis presupposes the naming theory, as statements like the following clearly show. *Language, Truth and Logic,* p. 124:
    "It should be clear, also, that there is no philosophical problem concerning the relationship of mind and matter other than the linguistic problems of defining certain symbols which denote logical constructions in terms of symbols which denote sense-contents."
12. Benjamin Lee Whorf, *Language, Thought, and Reality,* ed. by John B. Carroll

(Technology Press of Massachusetts Institute of Technology, 1956).

13. John Hospers, *Introduction to Philosophical Analysis* (Prentice-Hall, 1953).

14. Bertrand Russell, "The Philosophy of Logical Atomism," *The Monist*, 1918-1919.

15. One example is John Searle in *Speech Acts* (Cambridge University Press, 1970), Ch. 2. His development of J. L. Austin's notion of "illocution" in terms of "propositional act" completely undermines the value by returning to a representational, naming theory of speech acts.

16. Cf. the extensive quotation from Wittgenstein in Chapter 1, note 9.

17. Ayer in *Language, Truth and Logic*, p. 63:
    "What we are saying is that all the sentences in which the symbol *e* occurs can be translated into sentences which do not contain *e* itself, or any symbol which is synonymous with *e*, but do contain symbols b,c,d. . . . In such a case we say that *e* is a logical construction out of b,c,d. . . . And, in general, we may explain the nature of logical constructions by saying that the introduction of symbols which denote logical constructions is a device which enables us to state complicated propositions about the elements of these constructions in a relatively simple form."

18. For different statements of this criterion and its ramifications, see Ayer, *Language, Truth and Logic*, pp. 35-45; Hans Reichenbach, *The Rise of Scientific Philosophy* (University of California Press, 1958), Ch. 16; and James O. Urmson, *Philosophical Analysis* (Oxford: Clarendon Press, 1956), Chs. 6-8.

19. Cf. the Introduction to the Second Edition of Ayer, *Language, Truth and Logic;* Urmson, *Philosophical Analysis*, Ch. 8; and John Wisdom, *Paradox and Discovery* (Oxford: Basil Blackwell, Publishers, 1966), Ch. 6.

20. Ayer, *Language, Truth and Logic*, p. 62, and Wittgenstein, *Tractatus*, p. 151:
    "The correct method in philosophy would really be the following: to say nothing except what can be said, i.e. propositions of natural science—i.e. something that has nothing to do with philosophy—and then, whenever someone else wanted to say something metaphysical, to demonstrate to him that he had failed to give a meaning to certain signs in his propositions. Although it would not be satisfying to the other person—he would not have the feeling that we were teaching him philosophy—*this* method would be the only strictly correct one."

21. Gottlob Frege, *Translations from the Philosophical Writings of Gottlob Frege*, ed. by Peter Geach and Max Black (Oxford: Basil Blackwell, Publishers, 1970), p. 194:
    "Signs would hardly be useful if they did not serve the purpose of signifying the same thing repeatedly and in different contexts, while making evident that the same thing was meant."
    and Russell, *Logic and Knowledge*, p. 179:
    "You can, for instance, say: 'There are a number of people in this room at this moment.' That is obviously in some sense undeniable. But when you

come to try and define what this room is, and what it is for a person to be in a room, and how you are going to distinguish one person from another, and so forth, you find that what you have said is most fearfully vague and that you really do not know what you meant."

22. Russell speaks both for himself and for the early Wittgenstein when he writes in his Introduction to the *Tractatus*, p. x:

"A logically perfect language has rules of syntax which prevent nonsense, and has single symbols which always have a definite and unique meaning. Mr. Wittgenstein is concerned with the conditions for a logically perfect language—not that any language is logically perfect, or that we believe ourselves capable, here and now, of constructing a logically perfect language, but that the whole function of language is to have meaning, and it only fulfils this function in proportion as it approaches to the ideal language which we postulate."

Chapter 3. KNOWLEDGE BY INFERENCE

1. Ayer, *Language, Truth and Logic*, pp. 31 and 34-35.

2. Reichenbach, *The Rise of Scientific Philosophy*, and Wesley Salmon, "The Short Run," *Philosophy of Science*, Vol. 22 (1955), pp. 214-221.

3. Ayer, *Language, Truth and Logic*, p. 50:

"Thus it appears that there is no possible way of solving the problem of induction, as it is ordinarily conceived. And this means that it is a fictitious problem, since all genuine problems are at least theoretically capable of being solved: and the credit of natural science is not impaired by the fact that some philosophers continue to be pulled by it. Actually, we shall see that the only test to which a form of scientific procedure which satisfies the necessary condition of self-consistency is subject, is the test of its success in practice. We are entitled to have faith in our procedure just so long as it does the work which it is designed to do—that is, enables us to predict future experience, and so to control our environment."

Cf. also Bertrand Russell, *The Scientific Outlook* (London: Allen & Unwin, 1931), p. 67. "All scientific laws rest upon induction, which considered as a logical process, is open to doubt, and not capable of giving certainty."

4. See, for instance, how Spinoza *simply begins* by defining his key terms, and then proceeds to extract further concepts and propositions from them. (*The Rationalists*, pp. 179ff.) Specifically see Descartes, in *The Rationalists*, pp. 128ff.

5. Cf. Hume, *A Treatise of Human Nature*, Book I, Part IV, sec. IV.

6. Cf. Alfred J. Ayer, *The Foundations of Empirical Knowledge* (Macmillan Co., 1940), pp. 239-241.

7. Cf. René Descartes, *Meditations*, First Meditation.

8. Cf. Hume, *A Treatise of Human Nature*, Book I, Part IV, sec. I.

9. Kant, *Critique of Pure Reason,* "Transcendental Doctrine of Judgement (Phenomena and Noumena)," pp. 257-275.

10. Cf. "The Preamble" to Kant's *Prolegomena to Any Future Metaphysics.*

11. Cf. here the work of Wesley Salmon, especially, "Should We Attempt to Justify Induction?" *Philosophical Studies,* Vol. 8 (1957), pp. 33-48.

12. Pierre Simon de Laplace, *Treatise on Probability,* 1886.

13. In Jerry H. Gill (ed.), *Philosophy Today No. 3* (Macmillan Co., 1970).

14. Paul Feyerabend, *Against Method* (Minnesota Studies in the Philosophy of Science, University of Minnesota Press, 1960), and N. R. Hanson, *Patterns of Discovery* (Cambridge University Press, 1958).

15. Thomas Kuhn, *The Structure of Scientific Revolution* (University of Chicago Press, 1970).

16. Peter Berger and Thomas Luckmann, *The Social Construction of Reality* (Doubleday & Co., 1967).

17. Van A. Harvey, *The Historian and the Believer* (Macmillan Co., 1966; Westminster Press, 1981), especially Chs. 4 and 5.

18. John Locke, *An Essay Concerning Human Understanding* (London: Oxford University Press, 1934), Book IV, Ch. xix: "Entertain not any proposition with a greater assurance than the proofs it is built upon warrant."

19. W. K. Clifford, "The Ethics of Belief," in *Lectures and Essays,* ed. by F. Pollock, Vol. II (London, 1879).

20. Blaise Pascal, *Pensées,* #253-282.

Chapter 4. THE CONSEQUENCES FOR RELIGION

1. Nearly all traditional theologians and philosophers of religion followed this approach, whereas today only fundamentalists and evangelical thinkers can be said to do so.

2. Generally Deists of the Enlightenment and nineteenth-century liberals, such as Friedrich Schleiermacher. See the latter's *Speeches on Religion to Its Cultured Despisers* as an excellent case in point.

3. For a more thorough consideration of the difficulties inherent in *The Myth of God Incarnate,* ed. by John Hick (Westminster Press, 1977), see my "Myth and Incarnation," *The Christian Century,* Dec. 21, 1977.

4. This way of using religious and theological language is especially characteristic of Neo-Reformation thinkers such as Karl Barth (cf. *Church Dogmatics,* Vol. 1), Emil Brunner (cf. *Revelation and Reason*), and Reinhold Niebuhr (*The Nature and Destiny of Man*). It is also highly prevalant among contemporary conservative thinkers of the evangelical persuasion, such as Carl F. H. Henry, Helmut Thielicke, and G. C. Berkouwer.

5. The early empiricists, especially Hume, and Russell exemplify this traditional approach, as does Kant in a slightly more complex fashion. The quotations

from Kant which appear in Chapter 1, notes 3 and 17, make his way of treating God talk fairly plain.

6. Ayer's *Language, Truth and Logic* is, of course, the most well-known expression of this position (cf. especially Chs. 1 and 6). Wittgenstein's *Tractatus* also expresses this position, but shows considerable respect for such talk nonetheless (cf. especially pp. 145-151).

7. Both R. B. Braithwaite, *An Empiricist's View of the Nature of Religious Belief* (Cambridge University Press, 1955), and R. M. Hare, "Theology and Falsification," in *New Essays in Philosophical Theology,* ed. by Antony Flew and Alasdair MacIntyre (London: SCM Press, 1955).

8. John Hick is particularly well known for advocating what he calls "eschatological verification." See his *Faith and Knowledge*, 2d ed. (Cornell University Press, 1966).

9. Rudolf Bultmann, *Kerygma and Myth* (Harper & Row, 1961).

10. Paul Tillich, *Systematic Theology,* Vol. 1 (University of Chicago Press, 1951).

11. For a detailed critique of Tillich's position, see my "Paul Tillich's Religious Epistemology," *Religious Studies,* Spring, 1968.

12. For a profound and thorough critique of contemporary Empiricism, see Alan Pasch, *Experience and the Analytic* (University of Chicago Press, 1958).

Chapter 5. THE FABRIC OF EXPERIENCE

1. For a brief treatment of this contrast in the early and later work of Wittgenstein, see my "Wittgenstein and Metaphor," *Philosophy and Phenomenological Research,* Fall 1980.

2. This problem is evident in both the British empiricists (e.g., Locke and Hume) and the logical empiricists (e.g., Russell and Ayer). It is pinpointed especially well by Pasch in *Experience and the Analytic*.

3. Both Descartes and Kant overlook these difficulties. Once again Merleau-Ponty's critique is especially helpful: Maurice Merleau-Ponty, *The Phenomenology of Perception*, tr. by Colin Smith (Humanities Press, 1962), pp. 3-50.

4. Here I am drawing on the work of traditional Gestalt theorists (e.g., Wolfgang Kohler) as well as that of more recent researchers, James J. Gibson, *The Senses Considered as Perceptual Systems* (Houghton Mifflin Co., 1966), and Jerome S. Bruner, *On Knowing* (Atheneum Publishers, 1965).

5. See here Merleau-Ponty's discussion in *The Phenomenology of Perception*, pp. 203-368.

6. The current research here is well summarized by A. N. Meltzoff and M. K. Moore in *Science*, Vol. 198 (Oct. 1977), pp. 75-78.

7. Cf. Merleau-Ponty, *The Phenomenology of Perception*, pp. 98-147.

8. See especially Jean Piaget, *Six Psychological Studies,* tr. and ed. by David Elkind (Random House, 1968).

9. Pasch is especially helpful here, *Experience and the Analytic,* Chs. 3 and 4.

10. Peter F. Strawson's analysis in *Individuals* (London: Methuen & Co., 1964) provides a powerful documentation of this point.

11. Here I am drawing on the insights of social-interactionism as expressed in the work of George Herbert Mead, *Mind, Self, and Society,* ed. by Charles W. Morris (University of Chicago Press, 1952).

12. Pasch, *Experience and the Analytic,* p. 202.

Chapter 6. MEANING IN CONTEXT

1. Merleau-Ponty's discussion is especially helpful (*The Phenomenology of Perception,* Ch. 6, Part 1).

2. Here Heidegger's notion of language as "the house of Being" comes to mind. His later work stresses this cruciality of language to existence. Cf. Martin Heidegger, *Poetry, Language, Thought,* tr. by Albert Hofstadter (Harper & Row, 1971).

3. See Helen Keller, *Teacher* (Doubleday & Co., 1955).

4. Cf. Joseph H. Greenberg, *Anthropological Linguistics: An Introduction* (Random House, 1968).

5. Here I am drawing on the insights of the later Wittgenstein as developed in the early pages of his *Philosophical Investigations* (Macmillan Co., 1953).

6. I have in mind the endless discussions of such statements as "The cat is on the mat," "The present king of France is bald," etc. Critical philosophers write (and think!) as if statements have *a* meaning and as if this meaning somehow resides *in* the words independently of the way and place in which they are used.

7. The term is Kai Nielsen's, the view is that of Donald Hudson. See the former's article "Wittgensteinian Fideism," *Philosophy,* July 1969, and the latter's book, *Ludwig Wittgenstein* (John Knox Press, 1968).

8. It must not be assumed that all such cases are cases of deceit. We often speak vaguely in order to allow the other persons the "space" or freedom within which to make up their own mind or to discover something for themselves.

9. Wittgenstein, *Philosophical Investigations,* #107.

10. The term, as well as some of the insight, is borrowed from Pasch, *Experience and the Analytic,* Ch. 5.

11. Wittgenstein, *Philosophical Investigations,* #69-70.

12. Paul Edwards, "Professor Tillich's Confusions," *Mind,* April 1965.

13. For a profound critique of the critical view, see Owen Barfield, *Poetic Diction* (Wesleyan University Press, 1973), especially Chs. 3 and 4.

14. Here Max Black's insights are most helpful. See his *Models and Metaphors* (Cornell University Press, 1962).

15. Kuhn, *The Structure of Scientific Revolution.*

16. The relevant research, together with its implications, is presented in Joseph Church, *Language and the Discovery of Reality* (Random House, 1961).

17. Elizabeth Sewell, *The Orphic Voice* (Harper & Row, 1965).

Chapter 7. KNOWLEDGE THROUGH PARTICIPATION

1. The term and the insight are those of Michael Polanyi, *Knowledge and Being*, ed. by Marjorie Grene (University of Chicago Press, 1969), pp. 212-213ff.

2. See in this connection Marjorie Grene's *The Knower and the Known* (University of Chicago Press, 1969).

3. My way of doing this is based on the thought of Polanyi, but its particular form is my own. For more detailed explorations, see my "The Case for Tacit Knowledge," *The Southern Journal of Philosophy*, Spring 1971, and "On Knowing the Dancer from the Dance," *The Journal of Aesthetics and Art Criticism*, Dec. 1975.

4. Merleau-Ponty has also explicated the crucial role of the body in knowing (*The Phenomenology of Perception*, pp. 98-206).

5. Both Pasch (*Experience and the Analytic*) and Wittgenstein (*Philosophical Investigations*) make this point repeatedly and convincingly.

6. Polanyi zeroes in on this participatory dimension of knowing in his "*magnum opus*," *Personal Knowledge* (Harper & Row, 1958). Cf. especially Chs. 3 and 4.

7. Wittgenstein, *Philosophical Investigations*, #481.

8. Ludwig Wittgenstein, *On Certainty* (Oxford: Basil Blackwell, Publisher, 1963), #378.

9. Polanyi, *Personal Knowlege*, p. 312.

Chapter 8. POST-CRITICAL PHILOSOPHY

1. Wittgenstein, *On Certainty*, #471:
   "It is so difficult to find the beginning. Or, better: it is difficult to begin at the beginning. And not try to go further back."

2. Although this is not, perhaps, the best term, it is the one that has come to be used in characterizing the existentialist position. See William Barrett, *Irrational Man* (Doubleday & Co., 1958).

3. For a more detailed discussion of the connection between Kant and Kierkegaard, see my "Kant, Kierkegaard, and Religious Knowledge," *Philosophy and Phenomenological Research*, Dec. 1967.

4. I develop this interpretation at greater length in "Faith Is as Faith Does," in *Essays on Fear and Trembling*, ed. by Robert Perkins (University of Alabama Press, 1981).

5. I am partially indebted in this understanding of Kierkegaard to both Henry

Allison, "Christianity and Nonsense," in my *Essays on Kierkegaard* (Burgess Publishing Co., 1969), and Louis Mackey, *Kierkegaard: A Kind of Poet* (University of Pennsylvania Press, 1971).

6. Cf. Wittgenstein, *Philosophical Investigations*, #18:

"Do not be troubled by the fact that languages (2) and (8) consist only of orders. If you want to say that this shews them to be incomplete, ask yourself whether our language is complete;—whether it was so before the symbolism of chemistry and the notation of the infinitesimal calculus were incorporated in it; for these are, so to speak, suburbs of our language. (And how many houses or streets does it take before a town begins to be a town?) Our language can be seen as an ancient city: a maze of little streets and squares, of old and new houses, and of houses with additions from various periods; and this surrounded by a multitude of new boroughs with straight regular streets and uniform houses."

and Wittgenstein, *On Certainty*, #475:

"I want to regard man here as an animal; as a primitive being to which one grants instinct but not ratiocination. As a creature in a primitive state. Any logic good enough for a primitive means of communication needs no apology from us. Language did not emerge from some kind of ratiocination."

7. Cf. Wittgenstein, *Philosophical Investigations*, #217:

"How am I able to obey a rule?"—if this is not a question about causes, then it is about the justification for my following the rule in the way I do. If I have exhausted the justifications I have reached bedrock, and my spade is turned. Then I am inclined to say: 'This is simply what I do.' "

and Wittgenstein, *On Certainty*, #501:

"Am I not getting closer and closer to saying that in the end logic cannot be described? You must look at the practice of language, then you will see it."

8. Cf. my "Saying and Showing: Some Radical Themes in Wittgenstein's *On Certainty*," *Religious Studies*, Fall 1974.

9. Cf. my "Linguistic Phenomenology," *International Philosophical Quarterly*, Dec. 1973. The term is introduced by J. L. Austin in his essay "A Plea for Excuses," in *Philosophical Papers* (Oxford: Clarendon Press, 1961), p. 130.

10. Cf. my "Wittgenstein and Metaphor," *Philosophy and Phenomenological Research*, Fall 1980.

11. As was brought out in Chapter 7.

12. Cf. Edmund Husserl, *Phenomenology*, ed. by J. J. Kockelmans (Doubleday & Co., 1967).

13. Cf. Merleau-Ponty, *The Phenomenology of Perception*, Preface.

14. Heidegger is perhaps the most obvious case in point. Both his earlier, more existentialist writings and his later, more poetic works exhibit these qualities.

15. Cf. Merleau-Ponty's Preface to *The Phenomenology of Perception*, p. xiii.

16. Ibid., Part One.

Chapter 9. RELIGIOUS EXPERIENCE

1. A most helpful account of this dimensional understanding of experience is found in John Hick, *Faith and Knowledge*, Chs. 5 and 6.

2. Austin Farrer and John Macmurray have done a great deal to develop this general idea. See the former's *Finite and Infinite* (London: Dacre Press, 1960) and the latter's *The Self as Agent* (London: Faber & Faber, 1957).

3. Compare Gabriel Marcel's discussion of this distinction in his *The Philosophy of Existence* (Philosophical Library, 1949), Ch. 1.

4. Pascal, *Pensées, #233.*

5. I have in mind especially the work of George Herbert Mead, e.g., *George Herbert Mead on Social Psychology*, ed. by Anselm Strauss (University of Chicago Press, 1964), pp. 227-228:

> "Of course we are not only what is common to all: each one of the selves is different from everyone else; but there has to be such a common structure as I have sketched in order that we may be members of a community at all. We cannot be ourselves unless we are also members in whom there is a community of attitudes which control the attitudes of all. We cannot have rights unless we have common attitudes. That which we have acquired as self-conscious persons makes us members of society and gives us selves. Selves can only exist in definite relationships to other selves. No hard-and-fast line can be drawn between our own selves and the selves of others, since our own selves exist and enter as such into our experience only insofar as the selves of others exist and enter as such into our experience also. The individual possesses a self only in relation to the selves of the other members of his social group; and the structure of his self expresses or reflects the general behavior pattern of this social group to which he belongs, just as does the structure of the self of every other individual belonging to this social group."

6. Here see Berger and Luckmann, *The Social Construction of Reality.*

7. H. Richard Niebuhr's *The Responsible Self* (Harper & Row, 1963) provides an excellent analysis of this dynamic.

8. I have sought to work this out in more detail in my article "On Seeing Through a Glass, Darkly," *Christian Scholar's Review*, Dec. 1975.

9. I have developed this theme in an unpublished manuscript entitled "Jesus and the Old Soft-Shoe."

Chapter 10. RELIGIOUS LANGUAGE

1. Cf. Hans-Georg Gadamer, *Essays in Philosophical Hermeneutics* (University of California Press, 1976), pp. 62-63:

> "Rather, in all our knowledge of ourselves and in all knowledge of the world, we are always already encompassed by the language that is our own. We grow up, and we become acquainted with men and in the last analysis

with ourselves when we learn to speak. Learning to speak does not mean learning to use a pre-existent tool for designating a world already somehow familiar to us; it means acquiring a familiarity and acquaintance with the world itself and how it confronts us."

2. A reading of the original "classic" in this field, Flew and MacIntyre, *New Essays in Philosophical Theology*, should suffice to confirm this statement.

3. A first-rate development of this invocation can be found in John Wisdom, *Paradox and Discovery*.

4. Here again see Flew and MacIntyre, *New Essays in Philosophical Theology*. The most striking exception to this trend is the work of Ian Ramsey, which explores a wide variety of actual Biblical, creedal, and theological statements as the groundwork for further generalizations. See especially Ian Ramsey, *Religious Language* (Macmillan Co., 1957), *Christian Empiricism* (Wm. B. Eerdmans Publishing Co., 1974), and *Christian Discourse* (Oxford University Press, 1965).

5. One of the best defenses and developments of this understanding of metaphor is found in Max Black, *Models and Metaphors*.

6. I am drawing here from Paul Ricoeur's outstanding study, *The Rule of Metaphor* (Toronto: University of Toronto Press, 1977).

7. Ibid., Ch. 8.

8. Cf. John Wisdom's remarks in *Paradox and Discovery,* p. 124:

"One might have expected that in the sphere of religion everyone would have learned by now to move carefully and neither at once to accept nor hastily to reject what sounds bewildering. But no, even here we still find a tendency to reject strange statements with impatience, to turn from them as absurd or unprovable or to write them down as metaphor—deceptive or at best merely picturesque. Only a few months ago someone came to me troubled about the old but bewildering statement that Christ was both God and man. He had asked those who taught him theology how this could be true. Their answers had not satisfied him. I was not able to tell him what the doctrine means. But I did remind him that though some statements which seem self-contradictory are self-contradictory others are not, that indeed some of the most preposterous statements ever made have turned out to convey the most tremendous discoveries."

9. I am extrapolating here from Max Black's analysis of the way models function in theoretic discourse, *Models and Metaphors,* p. 238:

"We have seen that the successful model must be isomorphic with its domain of application. So there is a rational basis for using the model. In stretching the language by which the model is described in such a way as to fit the new domain, we pin our hopes upon the existence of a common structure in both fields. If the hope is fulfilled, there will have been an objective ground for the analogical transfer. For we call a mode of investigation rational when it has a rationale, that is to say, when we can find reasons which justify what we do and that allow for articulate appraisal and criticism. The putative isomorphism between model and field of application provides such a rationale and yields such standards of critical judgment. We can determine the validity of a given model by checking the extent of its isomorphism with its intended application. In appraising models as good or bad, we need not rely on the sheerly pragmatic test of fruitfulness in discovery; we can, in principle at least, determine the 'goodness' of their 'fit.' "

10. John Wisdom speaks forcefully to this point in *Paradox and Discovery*. See also Barfield, *Poetic Diction*, p. 86:

"Men do not invent those mysterious relations between separate external objects, and between objects and feelings or ideas, which it is the function of poetry to reveal. These relations exist independently, not indeed of Thought, but of any individual thinker. And according to whether the footsteps are echoed in primitive language or, later on, in the made metaphors of poets, we hear them after a different fashion and for different reasons. The language of primitive men reports them as direct perceptual experience. The speaker has observed a unity, and is not therefore himself conscious of relation. But we, in the development of consciousness, have lost the power to see this one as one. Our sophistication, like Odin's has cost us an eye; and now it is the language of poets, in so far as they create true metaphors, which must restore this unity conceptually, after it has been lost from perception."

11. Here I am drawing from Ian Ramsey's studies, especially *Religious Language* and *Christian Discourse*.

12. The work of Sallie McFague TeSelle is important here. See her *Speaking in Parables* (Fortress Press, 1975), pp. 5-6:

"The world of the parable, then, includes, it is, both dimensions—the secular and the religious, our world and God's love. It is not that the parable points to the unfamiliar but that it includes the unfamiliar within its boundaries. The unfamiliar (the kingdom of God) is the context, the interpretative framework, for understanding life in this world. We are not taken out of this world when we enter the world of the parable, but we find ourselves in a world that is itself two-dimensional, a world in which the 'religious' dimension comes to the 'secular' and reaffirms it."

13. See Austin, *Philosophical Papers*, especially Chs. 10 and 3.

14. Here see J. L. Austin, *How to Do Things with Words* (Harvard University Press, 1962), especially Chs. 8 through 12.

15. Cf. Donald Evans, *The Logic of Self-Involvement* (London: SCM Press, 1963); John Hutchison, "Language Analysis and Theology," *Journal of American Academy of Religion*, Dec. 1967; James McClendon, "Baptism as a Performative Sign," *Theology Today*, Oct. 1966.

16. Cf. Dewi Phillips, *The Concept of Prayer* (London: Routledge & Kegan Paul, 1965).

Chapter 11. RELIGIOUS KNOWLEDGE

1. I am relying here on the work of J. L. Austin in his essay "Other Minds," in *Philosophical Papers*.

2. The works of Max Black, *Models and Metaphors*, and Ian Ramsey, *Models and Mystery* (Oxford: Oxford University Press, 1964), have been especially helpful here.

3. Any reliable church history boom will display this dialectic. Also, Thomas Kuhn's *The Structure of Scientific Revolutions*, with its distinction between "normal" science which functions within a specific conceptual paradigm and "revolutionary science" based on following up an anomaly. Henri Bergson's *The Two Sources of Morality and Religion* (the static and the dynamic) is also very applicable here.

4. The book by Ernest Nagel and James Newman, *Gödel's Proof* (New York University Press, 1958), is especially helpful in coming to grips with the essence and implications of this problem.

5. Here Wittgenstein's *On Certainty* represents the last word as far as I am able to determine.

6. See especially in this regard Polanyi, *Personal Knowledge*, pp. 309ff.:
   "While compulsion by force or by neurotic obsession excludes responsibility, compulsion by universal intent establishes responsibility. The strain of this responsibility is the greater—other things being equal—the wider the range of alternatives left open to choice and the more conscientious the person responsible for the decision. While the choices in question are open to arbitrary egocentric decisions, a craving for the universal sustains a constructive effort and narrows down this discretion to the point where the agent making the decision finds that he cannot do otherwise. The freedom of the subjective person to do as he pleases is overruled by the freedom of the responsible person to act as he must."

7. James McClendon and James Smith, *Understanding Religious Convictions* (Notre Dame University Press, 1975), p. 183.

INDEX

INDEX

Analogy, 133-134
Analysis, 13, 37-38, 47, 111, 155-157
Anselm, 60
Aquinas, Thomas, 28, 32, 53, 60, 63, 157
Aristotle, 32, 39, 42, 90, 141, 157
Artificial languages, 41, 83-86, 159
Atomism, 20, 26, 29, 47, 55, 111, 117-118, 124, 155-157
Augustine, 28, 32, 53, 127, 157
Austin, J. L., 110, 112, 134, 138, 158, 164, 167-168
Ayer, Alfred J., 13, 20-22, 32, 36, 156-159, 161

Barfield, Owen, 162, 167
Barth, Karl, 160
Behaviorism, 22, 124
Berger, Peter, 160, 165
Berkeley, George, 23, 32, 157
Black, Max, 112, 162, 166, 168
Braithwaite, R. B., 161
Bruner, Jerome S., 161
Brunner, Emil, 160
Bultmann, Rudolf, 58, 127, 136, 161

Carnap, Rudolf, 41, 83
Clifford, W. K., 51, 160
Cognitivity, 36, 58, 64, 86-88, 135-136

Descartes, René, 13, 21-26, 32, 37, 42-59, 60, 103, 124, 155, 157, 159, 161

Doubt, 46
Dualism, 28-30, 53-54, 58-59, 67-68, 75-76, 103, 117-118, 124

Edwards, Paul, 86, 162
Embodiment, 23-24, 69-72, 80, 95, 125-127
Empiricism, 20, 23, 34, 42, 45, 47, 61, 63, 67, 69, 71, 104
Evans, Donald, 167
Existentialism, 14-15, 56-58, 62-64, 99, 105-109, 121
Experience, 10-30, 53-56, 67-76, 117-128

Faith, 56, 62-64, 107-109, 149, 163
Farrer, Austin, 165
Flew, Antony, 161, 166

Gadamer, Hans-Georg, 165
Gibson, James J., 161
God talk, 15, 56-59, 129-140
Gödel, Kurt, 150

Hare, R. M., 161
Hegel, G. W. F., 23, 107
Heidegger, Martin, 162, 164
Heisenberg, Werner, 51
Hick, John, 160, 161, 165
Holism, 69-70, 72-75
Hume, David, 13, 20-24, 32, 37, 43-46, 48-49, 98, 155-157, 159-160, 161